# Praise for *A Passiᵤ  ⌐ ᵤₚₗₑ*

This book does the impossible: it captures the most seminal ideas of one of the most influential educators of our generation. Not only does it transmit Avraham's ideas – it communicates them with Avraham's signature passion, stories, humour and love for the Jewish people. In doing so, it ensures that future generations will continue to be exposed to the wisdom of our teacher, Avraham. *-Rabbi Shoshana Boyd Gelfand, Director JHub, UK*

This book beautifully weaves the personal stories of Avraham Infeld to allow in-depth understanding of modern Jewish Peoplehood, which is anchored in the State of Israel. Infeld's larger-than-life presence and personality beam through the pages of this wonderfully insightful book that summarizes the work of one of the greatest teachers of our generation. *-Gidi Grinstein, Founder, the Reut Group; author, Flexigidity, Israel*

Jewish tradition teaches "that words that come from the heart enter into the hearts of others." In *A Passion for a People*, Avraham Infeld speaks from his heart and offers his Torah to us in its most profound sense. He tells us the story of his life, and shares the insights and teachings he has derived from a lifetime of experience. His love for the Jewish people and the moral messages Jewish traditions contain are expressed on every page of this book, and his humanity and *menschlichkeit* shines out in every sentence. Anyone who wants to know what the best of Judaism and the Jewish people can be should read this book. They will see the soul of Avraham Infeld and understand why he became and still serves as one of the most beloved and instructive teachers of our time. *-Rabbi David Ellenson, Director of the Schusterman Center for Israel Studies at Brandeis University; Chancellor Emeritus and Former President of Hebrew Union College-Jewish Institute of Religion*

Avraham Infeld is our minstrel of Jewish passion and purpose. This book is one of policy and intimacy. In it Avraham speaks to the "me" and the "we" that should be a part of each of us. His Jewishness is joyous, optimistic and meaningful, a formula ripe for our times. This is a must read, and a delightful read. It is pure Infeld. *-Richard M. Joel, President Emeritus, Yeshiva University*

Those of us blessed to know Avraham Infeld know what a powerhouse teacher, a grand soul, and an impassioned voice for Jewish belonging he remains. Throughout his storied career, he has made it his life work to awaken the sense of Jewish civilization as the life breath of the Jewish people. More than a set of doctrines or rituals, Judaism is the living soul of the Jews, with our hearts turned toward Jerusalem and Israel. He truly lives a Passion for a People, and in reading this magical book, you will get to taste that passion and to share it. -*Rabbi Dr. Bradley Shavit Artson, Roslyn and Abner Goldstine Dean's Chair, Ziegler School of Rabbinic Studies, American Jewish University*

*A Passion for a People* reflects Avraham's years of experience teaching and interacting with Jews of all ages and backgrounds. Avraham's passion and love of the Jews as a people comes through in each and every page in this book. The two areas that we as Jewish people need to rally around are the concept of ensuring unity without uniformity and that Israel remains the Nation-State of the Jewish people. Avraham does a masterful job in challenging us and offering a vision for the future. -*Jerry B. Silverman, President & CEO, the Jewish Federations of North America*

I believe the evidence will establish that Avraham Infeld has lectured to more Jewish young adults over the last several decades than any other contemporary Jewish educator, much of it through his deep and profound connection to Hillel. He is therefore one of the most influential Jewish voices of our generation, and without question one of the most beloved. In this book, Avraham shares the wisdom that he has been offering to his audiences, and many more insights from his personal history and global travels. If you want to know how to build a unified Jewish community in this critical moment in history, there is no better teacher to learn from than Avraham Infeld and there is no better place to start than this book. -*Eric Fingerhut, President & CEO of Hillel International*

From the moment I met Avraham, I knew I was in the presence of a special man. His dedication and commitment to the Jewish people are surpassed only by his love of Judaism itself. All who have had the opportunity to work with Avraham or, even better, to learn from him have been enriched by his spirit, his soul and his inspiring message. -*Shoshana S. Cardin, prominent international and national Jewish leader*

Master educator, raconteur extraordinaire and loving friend has finally written his first book. To no one's surprise, it is filled with wisdom and love for the Jewish people. A must read for all who feel bewildered by our present political leadership. Here we have a guide book to our better future. -*Brian Lurie, former President UJA, Immediate Past Chairman NIF*

Once in a generation, a book is published that becomes definitive for the Jewish people. *A Passion for a People* is such a book – it is nothing less than the book of our age. Beautifully written, incisive, and passionate, it will be talked about, argued over and debated across the Jewish world for years to come. Avraham Infeld has not only written a book unrivalled in its ability to inspire, but in doing so has written himself into the pantheon of those who have left a lasting imprint on the Jewish People. *-The Right Hon. Lord Jonathan Kestenbaum, House of Lords, UK*

In this fast-moving reflection on his decades as the premier global Jewish educator of our time, Avraham Infeld argues persuasively that "Judaism is NOT a religion." Drawing upon his persona, his passion, and his profession, he issues a call for Jewish Peoplehood education that rests on five key components: Memory, Family, Mount Sinai, Israel, and Hebrew. Not only is the work instructive and inspiring, but for a fracturing Jewish People, its analysis is insightful and its prescriptions are essential. *-Prof. Steven M. Cohen, New York and Jerusalem*

Avraham Infeld is a patriarch of our Jewish community. Like his Biblical namesake, he has pursued a prophetic vision with clarity, courage, and compassion. Hillel International, Birthright, and now Tikkun Olam Makers (TOM) bear his imprint. In this uplifting book, he harvests his story and our collective identity with warmth and wisdom, celebrating the Jewish people's dynamic future. *-Rabbi Elie Spitz, Congregational rabbi and author: Does the Soul Survive; Healing from Despair; Increasing Wholeness*

For decades, Avraham Infeld has been one of our most inspiring teachers. This memoir insightfully records how Infeld became the extraordinary Jew that he is. But this book is far more: it is a rich chronicle of how Jews young and old forge Jewish meaning and purpose navigating the full embrace of modernity. A must read for all working to strengthen the future of our people. *-John S. Ruskay, Executive Vice President emeritus of UJA-Federation of NY*

I enjoyed Avraham Infeld's book immensely. It is compelling, insightful and rich in wit. Yet beyond being a highly pleasurable read it is an important one. At a time when the threads that bind the Jewish people are unraveling, this book offers directions for re-weaving our people's connections. *-Micah Goodman, author, Maimonides and the Book That Changed Judaism, and Catch 67*

Like having an unforgettable week-end-long conversation with a charming friend, only that friend happens to be the big-hearted, brilliant Jewish educator, Avraham Infeld. His love of the Jewish people is an irresistible force. He teaches us through his treasure trove of stories and careful reasoning why being Jewish is about that love and how generous it can and must be. Over and over again we learn the blessings and the challenges of being "distinctively Jewish, universally human." We start to get it and then? We need to read it again and again until our hearts become as big as his.

-*Lee Meyerhoff Hendler, author,* The Year Mom Got Religion; *Chair, The Joseph and Harvey Meyerhoff Charitable Funds*

One of the truly original thinkers of our generation, Avraham has an unparalleled ability to use stories to bring millennia-old values and texts to life in terms the millennial generation – and everyone else – can grasp with amazing ease and comprehension. This book is more than the legacy of a great teacher, mentor, coach and friend to so many people – it is a roadmap to Jewish relevancy and meaning for the 21st Century and beyond.

-*Sandy Cardin, President, Charles & Lynn Schusterman Family Foundation*

*A Passion for a People* comprises a compelling and thought-provoking series of essays by an inspirational global Jewish leader and master educator. Infeld skillfully weaves together central Jewish ideas, traditional sources and personal anecdotes in a very unique manner. Small wonder he has profoundly impacted multiple students and colleagues whom include leading J educators of our generation. This highly informative and insightful work is a must read for all Jewish funders, leaders and professionals. -*Jonathan Mirvis PhD, author,* It's Our Challenge: A Social Entrepreneurship Approach to Jewish Education, *Senior Lecturer, the Hebrew University of Jerusalem*

Avraham Infeld has written a passionate and heartwarming love poem to and for the Jewish people. I could hear Avraham's earnest though playful voice bellowing throughout his personal and professional storytelling and reflections. His deep passion, vibrant vision, steadfast commitments, tikvah and optimism, and love for the Jewish people are inspirational and uplifting.

-*Saul Andron, PhD, Wurtzweiler School of Social Work, Yeshiva University*

# A Passion for a People

## Lessons from the Life
## of a Jewish Educator

### Avraham Infeld

with Clare Goldwater

We acknowledge with gratitude the permission granted us by The
Toby Press to reproduce the following two stories by S.Y. Agnon in the
appendix to this book: "Fable of a Goat" from *A Book That Was Lost*
and "From Foe to Friend" from *Forevermore and Other Stories*.

A Passion for a People: Lessons From the Life of a Jewish Educator
2017 Quality Hardcover Edition, First Printing

ISBN: 978-1-911175-95-7

Editor: Nikki Littman
Publisher: Melitz
Design: Jen Klor, Jerusalem

*To my wife Ellen,*
*our four children,*
*sixteen grandchildren,*
*our three great-grandchildren,*
*their future siblings, cousins and offspring.*

———

Feeling great
about being a part of
the Jewish People is a
wonderfully complex
and sublimely enriching
condition. It may also be
contagious – read this
book with caution
and a smile.

*Best wishes,*
*Avraham Infeld*

# Table of Contents

**Preface**
A Contemporary Wandering Magid (storyteller) –
Professor Gideon Shimoni     xi

**Introduction**
Building the Family     xv

**Part I: The Jews as a People**

1. The Jewish Future and the Jewish Past     3

2. Expanding Perspectives on Being Jewish     8

3. Memory and History – "Jews Don't Have History;
   Jews Have Memory"     15

4. Judaism is NOT a Religion! The Jews are a Family     25

5. God, Mount Sinai, and Being Right     39

6. Hebrew: The Language of the Jewish People     46

7. The Land of Israel: The Indigenous Home of the
   Jewish People     52

8. The State of Israel: A Balancing Act     60

9. America and Israel: Commonalities and Distinctions     74

**Part II: Peoplehood in Practice**

10. Teachers and Mentors     83

11. Educational Moments and Jewish Education     98

12. Hillel and Shammai: Models of Peoplehood
    Educators     108

13. Experiments in Jewish Peoplehood     112

**Part III: The Future of the Jewish People**

14. Future Challenges and Directions   127

   A. Ensuring Unity Without Uniformity – The Model of the 5 Legged Table   128

   B. Ensuring that Israel Remains the Nation-State of the Jewish People   132

   C. Re-Engineering the Infrastructure of the Jewish People: One Mission, Many Tasks   135

   D. Must Intermarriage Be Synonymous with Assimilation?   136

   E. Fulfilling Our True Mission: *Tikkun Olam*   137

**Appendices**

A: The Declaration of the State of Israel   141

B: Hillel and Shammai: Talmud Shabbat 31a   146

C: S.Y. Agnon Stories: "Fable of the Goat," and "From Foe to Friend"   150

**Acknowledgements**

Avraham Infeld   161

Clare Goldwater   164

Ami Infeld, CEO Melitz   166

Special Thanks   168

# Preface

# A Contemporary Wandering Magid (storyteller)

*Professor Gideon Shimoni, Hebrew University, Jerusalem*

As Avraham Infeld's own life story testifies, his Jewish family and community was its cradle. The country in which Aubrey, as he was then known, grew up in the 1950s was home to a vibrant Jewish community numbering some 100,000 Jews. Their situation was most unusual, perhaps even unique, in the experience of modern Jewish communities. For, in a racially divided society, wholly dominated by a minority who were Whites, they enjoyed all the democratic privileges, freedoms, and rights of citizenship. At the same time, their ethno-religious Jewish identity was greatly stimulated not only by the stringent racial division between the privileged Whites of European origin and the mainly African non-European majority, but even more so by the nationalist and cultural divisiveness within the White population itself between Afrikaners and people of mainly British origin.

Jewish ethnic identity, already strong by dint of the very homogeneous, mainly Litvak, origins of Jewish immigrants, was greatly augmented by this intra-White division. Jews could not become Afrikaners, not even if they spoke Afrikaans, nor could they integrate without social limitations within the English-speaking sector. Hence, the societal space between the two

White sectors left Jews room for their own distinctive and compelling ethnic identity. Its main expressions were Zionist both as sentiment and as a community institution. Consequently, in comparative Jewish community perspective, this community's most striking feature was the preeminence of Zionism. Indeed it may be said that the Zionist movement enjoyed hegemony in the organized life of South African Jewry, attaining its peak of vitality in the lead up to the creation of the State of Israel. This was precisely the period of Avraham's adolescence and the time when his beloved father, Zvi Infeld, occupied a key position in his capacity as director of the all-embracing South African Zionist Federation. So family and community were integral for young Avraham and hence the launching pad of his voyage into Zionist-motivated aliyah to Israel, and thence to the cause of Jewish "Peoplehood," a concept which became the hallmark of his famed educational enterprise.

This is not to say that religion had no part in the Jewish identity of South African Jews. Their Zionist movement included an orthodox religious component which never ever had to contend with any Ultra-Orthodox bodies such as constituted a powerful opposition to the Zionist movement in Europe. However, the normative pattern of Jewish religion in South Africa might most aptly be described as lightly observant or even non-observant Orthodoxy. This was the mode experienced by Avraham in his home and community prior to his coming to Israel, where a very different adversarial relationship separated the strictly Ultra-Orthodox from secularized or even moderately Orthodox Jews. Both the primacy of Zionism and this pattern of Jewish identity are reflected in Avraham Infeld's life. They have remained the basis upon which he pleads passionately for unity without uniformity and has developed his non-doctrinaire educational philosophy relating to Jewish identity, exemplified famously by his "Model of the 5 Legged Table."

To be sure, since Avraham left South Africa the Jews there have undergone a remarkable transformation which is not quite in tune with his approach. It has become a community in which strict Orthodox observance, attendant upon a politically right-wing identification, is increasingly prevalent. Yet this has not detracted much from its Zionist orientation. Although the Orthodox rabbinate has risen to a position of near-dominating authority in the life of the community, in contrast to the steep decline of all but the national-religious segment of the Zionist movement, it has subsumed rather than displaced popular Zionist sentiment and dedication to Israel.

Avraham grew up while the Afrikaner nationalist government was dogmatically enforcing its infamous apartheid system in the face of desperate but mainly non-violent opposition, which it proceeded to suppress. This raised grave moral dilemmas for Jewish community leaders, including Zvi Infeld. Some Jews chose to join the personally risky struggle against apartheid. However, the normative political stance adopted by the community's leadership, and upheld by most Jews, was a problematic policy of non-involvement, balanced by intensified Zionist identification, which for Zionist youth like Avraham meant personal aliyah to Israel.

Against this background, Avraham Infeld forged a unique path as an innovating role model in informal Jewish education. Transcending the formal academic sphere, in a sense Avraham Infeld has become what might be described as a contemporary equivalent of the traditional wandering magid. At the same time he created institutions – most notably Melitz – in an exponentially growing field of informal Jewish education aimed at shaping positive, plural Jewish identity world-wide although centered on Israel. In this way Infeld is a foremost advocate of Jewish peoplehood as a guiding concept and educational practice for contemporary Jewry.

There is a view that argues that emphasis on Jewish peoplehood is an evasion of true Zionism. This is not correct. Infeld's advocacy of peoplehood is entirely compatible with his roots in Zionist ideology, firmly premised on the proposition that the Jews are not to be defined essentially as adherents of a religion called Judaism. They are a people. "Wir sind ein Volk," declared Herzl in his seminal work Der Judenstaat. And it is as a people that they have a dire existential need and moral entitlement to national self-fulfillment in a state of their own, which in turn has central significance for Jewish life everywhere in the world. Emphasis on peoplehood merely broadens Zionism's tent of inclusiveness and plurality by averting out of date "negations of the Galut" that dismissed the validity or viability of all Jewish life outside Israel. Affirmation of peoplehood as the exponential expansion of a caring family that encompasses the plurality of Jewish life and unity in diversity is Avraham Infeld's message in this autobiographical book. It is a written supplement to his superbly communicative talks, which continue to inspire his many proteges and colleagues.

# Introduction

## Building the Family

In January 2016 I traveled to Vienna as the scholar in residence for a group of leaders from various Jewish Federations in North America. My job was to add some of my own thoughts after the guest speakers had left, schmooze with the participants, and generally add an educational lens to the program. On the last day, I thought I had finished with my responsibilities and made a plan to go looking for my grandfather's grave. I knew that he had died before World War II and was buried in Vienna, and I had asked around to see if his grave was documented and could be found. I learned that there was an Infeld buried in the Zentralfriedhof (Central Cemetery), so I told the group I was going to leave them and go looking for it. They insisted on coming with me, so we found ourselves walking through the enormous cemetery together.

There are more than three million people buried there, including the Jewish section, and the sections are old, overgrown, and totally chaotic. It is hard to read the gravestones or to find your way around, so it was enormously helpful that I had the help of the group, who fanned out looking for the grave of my grandfather. Suddenly one of them shouted "I've found it," and sure enough, there he was: Avraham Meir ben Rabbi Eliezer Infeld. My father's father, who died in 1924 at the age of 60, the father of nine children, and after whom I am named. I doubt that my father ever visited his own father's grave; I am probably the first of my generation to find their way there. To say *Kaddish* at his grave was an enormously powerful experience that closed the circle on many stories and longings that have accompanied my life. It was the culmination of a promise I had made to my father, and it embodied my commitment to family and memory.

When I told one of my grandsons about this experience and how this visit to my grandfather's grave somehow fit the pieces of my life together to form a coherent whole, he said, "*Saba*, now I understand what you do in your life. You build families. You build the big family and the small family. That is your profession. Now I understand everything."

My grandson is right. I am a builder – not of buildings but of families. I start with my own family, which today numbers my wife, our four children, 16 grandchildren, and three great-grandchildren; all of whom I am incredibly proud. And then I expand my perspective, yielding to the eternal pull that I feel toward the extended Jewish family: to those I don't know personally but I love anyway and to the relatives across time and space that Jewish history has bequeathed me.

I have dedicated my life to building families of all sizes and in all places where Jewish families live. These Jewish families are important to me because we are connected through our belonging to the Jewish People, and so my career has been dedicated to exploring, sharing, and developing the concept of Jewish Peoplehood. This has not been a simple undertaking. Most Jews find it easier and more fulfilling to define themselves as either a member of a religion or of a nation rather than a people, a fact that I find extremely frustrating. As you will see in the following chapters, I believe that both of these concepts fail to define all Jews and contribute only to divisiveness and confusion for all those trying to make sense of being Jewish. The only concept that is, to my mind, inclusive of all Jews is that of Peoplehood, yet that term (*Amiyut* in Hebrew) remains controversial, unfamiliar, and unused in many Jewish educational circles.

Perhaps some of the difficulty with the term Jewish Peoplehood is explained by the complexity of defining the base concept, "People." My friend and teacher Professor Gidi Shimoni of the Hebrew University has taught me that an acceptable definition of People is an ethnic group or "ethnos" – an expansion of the concept of tribe, which is, in turn, an expansion of the concept of family. Common to all of these frameworks is the emphasis on common ancestry, which is always true in the case of family and is sometimes true or perceived to be so as you expand outward. That is precisely who we the Jews are: a family that has expanded into an "ethnos," a group with a collective belief in a shared ancestry. Judaism is the culture of this ethnic group, a culture that has as its central motif the group's unique relationship with God. The presence of God in this story, however, does not make Judaism a religion. One cannot practice the Jewish religion without a sense of belonging to the People.

In this book, then, the protagonist is the Jewish People, with a supporting role played by God. The scenes take place in different venues, many of which are homes to Jews but only one of which is home to the entire Jewish People. When the curtain rises on the story in Part I, I introduce you to the childhood experiences that made me forever committed to the Jewish People; to the examples of our ongoing on-off love affair with God; to the eternally changing context in which Jewish life is lived; to the power of the language and the critical role played by the homeland; and to the collective memories that animate the people, wherever they are. In Part II I tell you about my attempts to put Peoplehood into action; about the teachers and mentors who have bequeathed me their wisdom; about the opportunities I have been given to test my ideas in varying institutions; and the educational approach that I have developed through experience. Finally, in Part III you learn about my hopes and dreams for the future of the Jewish People; the challenges that are facing us at this tremendously exciting period in our history; and the model of the 5 Legged Table, my recipe for the continued significant renaissance of the Jewish People. This book is a story of my love for the Jewish People and so, despite the inevitable lack of clarity and fog that remains, I want to inspire other Jews to join me in helping this confused and confusing, obviously not uniform but hopefully unified, global but tied-to-a-homeland Jewish People make their own particular contribution to perfecting the world.

This book is my first attempt to collect in written form the thoughts and teachings that are the fruit of my life's work. Some of them are familiar, and I speak about them all the time. Others have emerged in the course of working on this book, and I hope they will be new and challenging. The journey of writing this book hasn't been easy. I have always shared my ideas orally, through the medium of telling stories and with the active input and energy of an audience. Writing, for me, is a far more difficult undertaking. When I lecture I find it educationally helpful to use powerful and sometimes provocative statements such as "Judaism is not a religion!" "The Jews are a family," or "Being Jewish demands combining an ethnic with an ethic." For those who have heard me lecture, these statements are usually repeated passionately, fortified by audience reaction and interaction. I strongly believe in all these statements, but when presented in the written form some of their nuance and power is lost, and they could be construed, without this introduction, as unfounded or illogical slogans. Nevertheless, I have continued to use many of these statements in the book and beseech my readers to understand them as deeply-held beliefs that are intended to provoke, stimulate, and entertain rather than as philosophical statements to be defended using academic-style justifications and footnotes.

How do you turn a life's work and experience into under 200 pages? And what will happen if I change my mind tomorrow? After all, I am not an academic or theoretician; I am a storyteller, a teacher, a passionate member of the Jewish People. I don't come with a comprehensive theory but rather with thoughts on a wide range of related topics, so that Jewish leaders, educators, and passionate Jews can engage with these ideas, debate them, and create their own dreams out of them. Through the stories and the ideas that emerge from them I highlight the many paradoxes that I see around me in Israel and the Jewish world, and describe how engaging with those paradoxes has provoked me to develop new paradigms for understanding and ways of thinking.

Even though I have had a long and productive career, I still feel young enough to have hopes and dreams for the future. I have heard it said (by my friend Micah Goodman who attributed it to the late Shimon Peres), that a person is still young when their dreams, hopes, and challenges are larger than their memories. Being old means that your memories make up most of who you are. For me, as you will see in the chapters that follow, memories are very central, but I still have so many dreams and hopes for what can be changed in the Jewish world. This book is my attempt to share both the memories and the hopes for addressing our challenges.

I truly hope that the ideas contained here will introduce new concepts, deepen familiar ideas, and add a personal perspective drawn from my life's lessons. The ideas do not end with this book. Rather, I look forward to continuing developing them – through *The 5 Legged Table* and Melitz – with educators, community leaders, and interested Jews from all over the world.

# Part 1

## The Jews as a People

# 1

## The Jewish Future and the Jewish Past

It is a fascinating paradox that the Hebrew word *kadimah*, which means moving forward, comes from the same root letters as *kodem*, which means before or behind. From this we gain the critical insight that the ability to move forward is integrally connected to what is behind us: we can't move in the right direction toward the future unless we properly recognize and understand our past.

My past is our shared, collective Jewish past. I was born to a Jewish People who were slaves in Egypt, stopped for an important event at Mount Sinai, settled in the Land of Israel where we built a Temple and a commonwealth, were exiled and returned from exile, and were exiled again as punishment for bad behavior but with a promise for a future return. Generations and generations of my People waited for God to send them the Messiah, and while they were waiting, they built thriving communities and developed a rich literature-based culture that embodied collective memories and values. The Messiah never (yet) came though; instead, they confronted another "m" – modernity – and that changed everything.

Modernity, which led to the political emancipation of the Jews of Europe, was a hugely disruptive event in Jewish life. In the pre-modern world, while there had always been debates about how to observe Judaism, there was at least uniformity about what it meant to be a Jew – namely, a member of a people who are born to Jewish mothers and share common memories, including a particular relationship with a universal God. Being a Jew also meant sharing an understanding of the past and the future, which included a return to the Land of Israel and an (albeit undefined) expectation of redemption.

Meeting modernity, however, shattered this uniformity. Our very understanding of what it meant to be a Jew was totally disrupted, and Jews took new directions in life in response to the shock of the Emancipation. Some chose to assimilate out of Jewish life and into surrounding cultures, and they were mostly successful until anti-Semitism forced them to choose other options, such as retreating into the ghetto and closing the gates behind them. Others chose to redefine Judaism, not as a people but as a religion. One further option became modern nationalism in a Jewish form, which eventually led to the establishment of the State of Israel. Jews who moved out of the ghetto and into mainstream societies found themselves most welcomed as a religious group by societies with respect for religious minorities. This was particularly true for American Jews, who adopted Judaism as a religion and not as a people and found enormous success in America, founded as it is on the principle of freedom of religion.

Responses to the Emancipation were successful in their own terms. However, despite their common starting point, Jews in the post-Emancipation world are no longer uniform, neither in practice nor in the basic definition of what it means to be a Jew. We no longer have a shared set of understandings about who a Jew is or what a Jew does; we no longer recognize each other as valuable members of the family. We have split into subtribes – the Zionist, the Haredi (ultra-orthodox), the assimilated Jew, and the denominational Jew – each with its own definition of what it means to be a Jew. The question then is: How can we be unified when we are not uniform? In my opinion, the Jewish People cannot survive as a people without being unified. We therefore have to come up with an approach to Jewish life that aspires to unity but without the uniformity of the pre-modern era. We cannot turn back the clock, even if we want to; modernity is the reality into which we were born. My great-grandfather was waiting for the Messiah in the ghetto. My grandfather was teetering on the brink – he didn't know which way to go – so he moved from Poland to Vienna. My father decided that the Messiah wasn't coming after all and took things into his own hands by building the State of Israel. I was born after that, after everything that had gone before, and I cannot accept disunity as an inevitable result of our history.

Later I describe in more detail how my understanding of being Jewish today has been continually enriched by the multiplicity of modern Jewish identities that I have encountered. To my secular Zionist perspective, I added a religious component; to my Orthodox practice, I added an appreciation of liberal Judaism; to my sense of the Jewish People as a majority nation, I added an awareness of Jews as a religious minority. Each time, rather than replacing what came before with a new, improved version, I added layer upon layer of meaning about what being Jewish means to me. The *tsimmes* – my own stew of Jewish identity – has become richer and tastier over time. And the assumption behind it is very important – namely, there cannot be a single way or truth for what it means to be Jewish; there are only multiple perspectives on the same truth. Some choose to be religious Jews, others are nationalist Jews (sometimes we call them Zionists), others still are Haredim. And while it is each person's responsibility to find a Jewish expression that is right for them, it is also crucial that we create a foundation upon which we can be unified. This is critical in a post-Emancipation and postmodern world.

However, there are risks that accompany this approach. First, while it allows for many access points for numerous people, it runs the risk of creating so many customized versions of Jewish identity that we will find ourselves with nothing in common. Instead of all eating from the same pot of *tsimmes*, we will be busy cooking our own and never sharing! Second, this approach puts no limits on what is considered acceptable as Jewish expression. Is everything really acceptable? I don't think so. I believe there are limits to what should be part of Jewish expression and practice. While I may pray every morning, learn the daily Talmud page, and only eat kosher food, that is right for me but not necessarily for you. So, how do you determine what is right for you? I suggest a series of questions that determine whether innovations in Jewish life are worthy of becoming part of the norms and collective memory of the Jewish family:

1. Does this practice or idea aim for unity and common purpose? Does it build something new out of the building blocks – the memories, customs, and values – that Jews have been using for centuries? Will we be more united and enriched as a family by these new ideas?

2. Is this practice or idea really meaningful? What makes it significant? What are the regular practices, language, and culture that will sustain it and keep its significance alive? How will it be transferred to others?

I believe that in order to engage meaningfully with these questions, it is necessary to understand and appreciate the building blocks have been the constituent components of Jewish Peoplehood for generations: our language, our particular relationship with God, our homeland, and more. In Part I of this book, the chapters describe how my experiences have led me to my approach to Jewish Peoplehood and how I understand its varied components and the elements that give this People its character and identity, its diversity, and its message to the world.

# 2

# Expanding Perspectives on Being Jewish

*I was once giving a lecture in Los Angeles, and
it was arranged that before the lecture I would
go to the house of some local people for dinner.
They were a Conservative Jewish family with
a kosher home. They were vegetarian and had
adopted two children whom they had converted
to Judaism. While we were having dinner, the
children were playing in the garden with some
friends. At one point, the six-year-old ran into
the house and asked, "Abba, I don't remember
why we don't turn on lights on Shabbat. Is
it because we are vegetarian, because we are
converted, or because we are adopted?" Identity
is, as we know, a serious and complicated
business!*

Judaism was embedded in the fabric of my life as a child growing up in Johannesburg, South Africa of the 1940s and 1950s.
It was a way of being that encompassed everything; it defined
my friends, the holidays we celebrated, and the languages spoken in my house. Just like the six-year-old in Los Angeles, all
the components of my identity were holistically connected. I
couldn't separate or isolate them. Being Jewish was the totality
of my identity, and as a result it was deeply felt and invisible to
me, in the way that our family's behaviors often are, until we
experience something else and suddenly realize that there are
other possibilities out there. In my case, it turns out that my
family's way of being Jewish was not typical of other South African Jews. Rather, it was highly idiosyncratic, the product of
parents who were neither South African natives nor Lithuanian
immigrants like the rest of the community. My parents viewed
themselves as temporary residents in South Africa, serving the
Jewish community on behalf of the Zionist movement.

My father, Zvi, was born in Galicia into a Hasidic family,
was seduced by the passion of modern, secular Zionism, and
spent most of his life as a Zionist activist and teacher, first in
Bulgaria and then South Africa. My mother, Olga, was born
in Poland and made *aliyah* to Israel, where she was recruited
by Zvi Infeld to be a Hebrew teacher in Sofia, Bulgaria. For
me, the deep imprints of Jewish life that I received in their
household from an early age remain the core of how I still see
Jewishness today, even as I have formed new paradigms for
myself over the years.

Our Shabbat was a good example of the eclectic mix of
observance and knowledge that my father embodied and that
defined our family. As a dedicated secularist, my father felt no
obligation to say particular prayers at a particular time, nor did
he refrain from activities prohibited by Jewish law. At the same
time, Shabbat was a profoundly Jewish time for us, with its
own particular feel and rhythm. On Shabbat morning I used

to go shopping with my mother or to a Saturday morning film with my cousin. Then, after lunch, my father would take out the Talmud and learn with me, without a *kippah* on his head and with a cigarette in his mouth; he didn't follow the religious laws against lighting a match on Shabbat, even though he was studying Talmud. He had learned Talmud as a young man, and he loved it. For my father, the Talmud was an ongoing conversation between Jews across time and space; it embodied Jewish culture and carried Jewish language in the broadest possible sense. He chose sections for us to learn that he believed were most relevant for the times: sections about civil laws or about the Land of Israel. He translated ancient issues into modern terms; for him, the passages in the tractate of Baba Kama about the owner of an ox that causes damage to its neighbor's property were directly comparable to a driver who had caused a car accident. He left out the legal discussions and commandments and focused on what he thought was most relevant to contemporary Jewish life. After we had learned Talmud, we would move to the living room, and he would put some opera on the record player. As the music was playing, my father described what would be happening on stage. I thus learned to appreciate and visualize opera, even though I had never seen one. This was my father's routine reserved for Shabbat, a time in which my father sanctified the two things he valued most highly. A love of both Talmud and opera are still with me today.

To celebrate the holiday of Shavuot I walked around the dining room table, dressed in white, carrying a basket filled with fruit, singing the classic Zionist song of the kibbutz movement, "We brought *bikurim* (the first fruits)!" That built a powerful memory for me, connecting me to the Zionist pioneers who were celebrating the harvest in Israel and to the extended Jewish People who were celebrating around the world. I was bringing my first fruits together with the rest of the Jewish People, even though they were, ironically, the wrong fruit! It is winter in South Africa at the time of Shavuot, so while my cousins in Israel were bringing figs and grapes as their bikurim, my basket was filled with apples, pears, and oranges. For our family, Shavuot was an agricultural festival that had been revitalized by the Zionist movement. I had no idea that Jews around the world celebrate Shavuot as the day on which the Torah was given. For me, it was simply the day when "we brought *bikurim*."

This was the Judaism I grew up with. It was central to my life; a secular, ethnic, Zionist form of Jewishness that I experienced as all-encompassing and totally normal, and my subsequent Jewish life has been built on this foundation. Each time I have encountered Jewish expression that differs from my parents' house, it has caused me to stand back and take notice. The first times this happened to me were pivotal experiences of my childhood, making me ask fundamental questions about Judaism and my father's approach to it.

My father loved telling me stories about his childhood. Together we chuckled as he told me how every morning his father would tie a knot in the straps of his *tefillin* (phylacteries) before he went to work, so that he could later check whether my father had put on *tefillin*. As he got older and rejected religious observance, my father would sometimes just untie the knot, so that my grandfather wouldn't know that he hadn't used his *tefillin*! When I was around 15 years old, I needed some money to buy a pair of homing pigeons. My father sent me to his desk – the same desk that sits in my study today – to find a small box at the back which contained some coins. And right at the back of the desk I found my father's *tefillin* with a knot in the straps that my grandfather had tied more than 40 years earlier! My father had not used the tefillin since; he didn't even remember they were there.

Finding the forgotten *tefillin* was a profound moment of

education for me. How come these little boxes were so important to my grandfather that he used to beat his son for not using them? And yet, they were so unimportant to my father that he never used them or gave them to me, but just kept them at the back of the drawer with a knot still in the straps. And if *tefillin* were so important to some Jews, how could my father have managed to create within me such a strong feeling of being a Jew, without them? The paradox of the *tefillin* in the back of the desk made me fundamentally question what it meant to be Jewish.

Around the same time, I encountered a teacher who exposed me to a totally different way of being Jewish. His name was Rabbi David Sanders, and I met him on a Sunday morning on my way to the swimming pool. I was on a street near my house and put out my hand to get a ride (as you did then in Johannesburg). An American guy wearing a *kippah* stopped to give me a ride. He asked me where I went to school and whether I had heard of the Talmud. "Yes, I am in the middle of Masechet Shabbat," I told him. He put out his hand, "I am David Sanders from Telz Yeshiva in America, and I have come over here to start a yeshiva. Do you want to come?" I didn't know what a yeshiva was, but I knew of some boys who went there, and Rabbi Sanders was a really great guy and married to a friend of my sister. So I went, and as I started to learn, I became interested in the religious aspects of Judaism, which were totally new to me. It was at the yeshiva that I learned the other parts of the Talmud that my father had left out: the legal sections that deal with *mitzvot* (commandments) and Temple rituals. And it was through this exposure that I discovered what religious Jews had known all along – namely, that being Jewish was about commandments and observance and that Shavuot was not only the secular agricultural holiday that I knew but also a celebration of the giving of the Torah. David Sanders showed me this religious component of Judaism, and I fell in love with it. It was a thickening of what I already knew about Jewish life, and it gave me more ways to be Jewish. My mother thought it was a passing phase, a rebellion, but it never passed because it brought me closer to more Jews in more places.

The ultimate understanding I attained from these contradictory experiences was that there is, without doubt, more than one way to be a deeply passionate Jew. If, even within my own family, there was evidence of multiple expressions of a powerful and passionate Jewish life, there must be more out there, and it became my mission to find as many ways of being Jewish as possible and participate in them all.

Just as my father looked for his way of being Jewish, I have looked for mine. And it turned out that my way is a little bit of everyone's way. Not only are there multiple ways to be Jewish, but encountering all those ways leads to a continually enriching perspective. My way of being Jewish is, in some ways, different from that of my parents. Some would see my religious observance as a repudiation of my parents' secular Zionist approach. I do not see it like that. I see myself as adding to what originally existed, with no need to totally replace it. For me, the return to observance is a fantastic opportunity to add an additional perspective, to incorporate another possibility into my current way of seeing things. I believe that the concept of *teshuva* allows us to say, "I have learned something new, which will enable me to see and do things differently in the future." And that is exactly what I have done. Each time I encountered something new in Judaism, I incorporated part of it into who I am. It didn't teach me that I was wrong before and now I was right – which is why my parents didn't have to worry that I would reject their Jewishness; rather, I took from the new experience and added it to what was already there. Thus, throughout my life, I have added new paradigms to old.

Every year for Rosh Hashana I like to make *tsimmes*, the traditional stew with a sweet flavor for a sweet new year. As I stir the *tsimmes*, I add the flour and watch the gravy get thicker and thicker. Every time I add something new, it adds a layer of richness to the whole stew; it doesn't take anything away. Perhaps it becomes a little chaotic at some point, but that is what I love! I love and appreciate each additional ingredient that brings new taste to the pot, more complexity to what it means to be Jewish. That is what culture is all about: building something slowly so that it incorporates as many people and as many ideas as possible. This is my way to fulfill my destiny. I was born into this group, and now it is my job to fulfill my potential to its maximum.

From an educational perspective, the principle I have learned through my own experience is that there is no single truth about how to be Jewish. Rather, there are multiple perspectives on a basic truth. How we see that truth is a function of our particular perspective at the time and the place we stand in history. My father had a perspective on the truth, Rabbi Sanders had a perspective on the truth, and while I struggled very hard to incorporate them, I didn't invent a new truth. My essence is that I am the son of Zvi and Olga Infeld and that I took something from all the additional perspectives to develop my own. As educators we must help our students do the same. They will end up looking different from us, but provided they have access to the various components of Jewish Peoplehood, they will find their own personal way of expressing their belonging to the Jewish People while maintaining some unity with other members of the extended family.

# 3

# Memory and History – "Jews Don't Have History; Jews Have Memory"

*When I arrived in Israel in my late teens, I decided to study at the Hebrew University. We have a few physicists in my family: my uncle was a famous physicist, my cousin was a professor of physics at Oxford, and, from the day I was born, my father knew that I was going to be the greatest physicist the world had ever seen. So, when I arrived at the Hebrew University, I registered to study physics. That was the plan.*

*On the first day of school I was walking toward the physics department, and all of a sudden I saw an extremely beautiful young lady walking toward the history department... so I decided to major in Jewish history instead... and today, she is the great-grandmother of my great-grandchildren!*

*I just had to explain the change of plan to my father. I sent him a letter and, in those pre-digital days, I got a telex back, greatly annoyed. Not with me, but with the Hebrew University. "What??" he wrote, "the Hebrew University has a department of Jewish history! Are they crazy! There is no such thing as Jewish history! Jews don't have history. We Jews have memory!"*

Today I know that my father was 100% correct. Memory and history are related but not the same, and memory is the base of Jewish identity. Who is a Jew? A Jew is a person who remembers what happened to the Jewish People in the past; a Jew is a person who is strictly forbidden from suffering long-term memory loss!

## History Versus Memory

Memory is sometimes confused with history, but they are, I believe, very different concepts. History is knowing what happened in the past; memory is asking yourself what those past events have to do with you today and tomorrow? If history is prose, memory is poetry. And like good poetry, memory is not necessarily dependent on facts. While history is regulated, on the whole, by the need to prove facts, memory is not constrained by them. Sometimes we remember things that might not have actually happened, but that does not diminish the value or the truth of the memory. Did the Exodus from Egypt actually happen? What are the facts around the destruction of the Temple in Jerusalem? Archaeologists and historians can argue over the evidence and come to various conclusions. For us as Jews, however, their conclusions are irrelevant. We know that the memory of the Exodus from Egypt is real and continues to be meaningful. We appreciate the care with which the Rabbis of the Talmud constructed Jewish life after the Temple's destruction so that we should remember specific values.

## Memory in Hebrew – *Zakhor*

We know that memory is central, because the Hebrew word for memory appears so often in the Torah. *Zikaron, zekher, zakhor* – the same Hebrew root in different forms is repeated throughout the Torah, commanding us over and over, to remember, remember, remember! One of the most paradoxical uses of the word is in relation to Amalek, the quintessential enemy of the Jewish People, whose army attacked the Israelites on their way out of Egypt, when they were weak and defenseless. The Torah says: "And the Lord said to Moses: Write this as a memorial (*zikaron*) in the book and rehearse it in the ears of Joshua; for I will utterly blot out the memory (*zekher*) of Amalek from under heaven" (Exodus 17:14). This is rather confusing. Is the memory of Amalek supposed to disappear from the world? If so, doesn't writing it down in a book achieve the opposite? That is the paradox of memory. For something as important as the eternal lesson of Amalek, it is critical to remember it, to be reminded of it on a regular basis. In fact, every Jew is commanded to listen to the story of Amalek every year, making sure that the memory stays fresh and relevant. Yet, Amalek is such a horrible memory, we would rather stamp it out. So, paradoxically, and with full knowledge of the irony, we have to both remember and forget at the same time. This is Jewish memory at its most deliberate and powerful.

On a recent trip to South Africa I encountered its post-apartheid challenge of how to deal with the central concept of memory when it is so busy trying to educate toward forgetting. South Africa is trying to forget its own painful past so that it can forge a shared future. But that is wrong! We Jews know that, just as in the case of Amalek, we have to remember AND forget in order to move forward. Instead of building different interpretations of a common memory, the South Africans are trying to erase the memory. They have much to learn from the Jewish experience.

## Core Jewish Memories

There are many memories that are central to our self-definition as Jews and to our ongoing Jewish lives. Once we start paying attention to the power of memory and the conscious ways that Jewish life invokes memory through all its rituals, holidays and stories, we find it everywhere.

### The origin story:
### *Abraham and the purpose of the Jewish People*

A group of core memories of the Jewish People surrounds our origins and purpose as a people. According to our tradition, humanity traces its roots back to Adam, but it wasn't until Abraham came along, generations later, that Judaism was born. Abraham separated himself from the idol-worshipping culture around him and said, "*ivri anochi*" (I am a Hebrew) to distinguish himself from the rest of his society. The word *ivri* comes from the root *e'ver*, which means on the other side. The word ivri thus contains within it the very notion of distinctiveness and being separated from something. The first Hebrew family and their descendants embody distinctiveness in their very being.

Abraham's act of circumcision, first of himself and then of his sons, Isaac and Ishmael, is a memory that we continue to reenact every time a boy is born into the Jewish family. The words of the blessing that a father says as he brings his son to be circumcised are a clear statement connecting him, and indeed the whole community, to the past: "to bring in [the infant] into the covenant of Abraham our father."

## Slavery and Exodus

One of our most powerful and long-lasting collective memories is the story of our slavery and exodus from Egypt. This story forms the spine of all our Jewish memories, and we have very specific and detailed instructions for keeping it alive. For generations we have sat down every year for a Passover *seder* to retell the story and remember the events described in the Torah. We are told in the Haggadah that: "Every Jew is commanded to see themself as if they had left Egypt." In other words, we don't want to have just a vague recollection of what happened to other people in Egypt; we actually want that memory to be our own memory, as if we had actually been there.

The collective memory of slavery demonstrates how memory turns facts into values and action. The memory of our being strangers in the land of Egypt turns the fact of our slavery into a value with practical application for our behavior today, namely: "Do not oppress the stranger...for you were strangers in the land of Egypt" (Exodus 23:9 and others).

## Mount Sinai

You and I met at Mount Sinai! Whether or not it ever happened, we stood there together! I always say this in my speeches, because that memory, the memory of our assembly at Mount Sinai, is a core memory for the Jewish People. We didn't leave Egypt and just end up in Israel. We stopped off at Mount Sinai, and something happened there, something that we remember to this very day. At Mount Sinai we, as a people, entered into a covenant with God and printed the visiting card that defines who we are, what our dreams are, and the nature of our relationship with God.

## Ephraim and Menashe

Every Friday night, at the Shabbat table, it is traditional for parents to bless their children. Boys and girls are blessed in the names of the patriarchs and matriarchs of the Bible, who embody core values that we want to remember. While girls are blessed, predictably, to embody the virtues of the four mothers, Sarah, Rebecca, Rachel, and Leah, it is interesting that we connect boys to Ephraim and Menashe, the grandchildren of Jacob, and not the three fathers, Abraham, Isaac, and Jacob. What is it about Ephraim and Menashe that we are trying to remember? There are several answers to this question, and each gives life to a different memory. Rabbi Samson Raphael Hirsch pointed out that Ephraim and Menashe grew up in Egypt as the sons of Joseph, the regent to Pharaoh. In contrast to Abraham, Isaac and Jacob, their life experience was as Jews in a non-Jewish world, in a society in which it was very easy to assimilate. Yet, despite this, they maintained their connection to Judaism and its values and were not drawn into pagan culture. Another answer focuses on the fact that, in contrast to the generations of the earlier patriarchs, they were the first generation of brothers to have peace between them, and so we choose to remember the positive potential of sibling relationships.

## The Exile

Since the destruction of the First Temple in 586 BCE, the traumatic experience of exile has been deeply imprinted on our collective consciousness. Even though we have experienced short periods of return to our land and to sovereignty, our collective memory continues to remind us of the pain of banishment and reenact the experience of being an outcast from our homeland. Our memories of exile are renewed every time we break a glass at a wedding and build a new house leaving a space undecorated, as well as in innumerable poems, prayers, and songs. Other peoples have envied our ability to continually commemorate and keep the reality of exile alive.

## The Holocaust

For me, the memory of the Holocaust is both central and peripheral at the same time. My grandmother and many other relatives were killed in Belzec. I live this experience as a core memory; likewise, many Jews today, especially Israelis, experience the Holocaust as a central Jewish memory. This is probably inevitable and may be necessary, given that the Holocaust was an unprecedented tragedy in our history. However, I am terrified of building a Jewish educational system around the memory of the Holocaust because of the messages that are associated with that memory: you must remain a member of the family because they hated us and killed us. This is not the message to learn from the Holocaust. Rather, we should be learning: Look what happened to a people who didn't have power. And look what happened to a people who did have power! Be aware and beware! The Holocaust reminds us of both the imperative of and the dangers of having power. It shows us the danger of dehumanization and the obligation to make the world a better place. It needs to be given its appropriate place among the collective memories of the Jewish People.

## Inculcating and Activating Memories

One of the most significant educational questions that we are dealing with today is how to inculcate memories into Jews who didn't grow up with them. How does a person gain a memory that wasn't theirs but that belongs to their people? And how do you help the non-Jewish partners of Jews to understand the memories that their partners are carrying? I believe that memory is taught and created; it isn't inherent. Ideally, it emerges from the slow process of absorbing songs, stories, concepts, and language. Even once you have absorbed the memory, keeping it alive is a very active pursuit. Memories that are not regularly revisited will die and lose their power. So we reinvigorate and revisit them through creating and telling stories, again and again. As I learned from my friend Zvi Bekerman, it is important to pay attention to the stories you tell your children. When you tell them about someone who took off their shoe, what do you want their associations to be? Cinderella or Moses at the burning bush?

## Storytelling for Memory-Building

Jewish civilization (like all other civilizations) has used stories, starting with the Torah and continuing through the Talmud and *midrashim* (rabbinic legends) all the way to contemporary music and poetry, to tell and retell our narratives. These narratives are not "just" stories making us feel good or providing us with entertainment. Their purpose is far greater than this. Rabbi Jonathan Sacks described what narratives do for us:

> Narrative connects children to something larger than themselves. It helps them make sense of how they fit into the world that existed before they were born. It gives them the starting-point of an identity. That in turn becomes the basis of confidence. It enables children to say: This is who I am. This is the story of which I am a part. These are the people who came before me and whose descendant I am. These are the roots of which I am the stem reaching upward toward the sun.
>
> (www.rabbisacks.org/the-spiritual-child-bo-5776/)

And this is not all. The stories also provide us with prescriptions for our future actions and interactions in the world. They are an important educational tool, as I describe in more detail later in Part II when I relate to the work of the educator.

## Pluralism and Assimilation

One of the beauties of a core memory is that it can be interpreted in many ways. Just look at the incredible variety of Haggadot that are published each year for Passover, each with its own particular approach and focus, to see how one single story can be interpreted with enormous variety. This testifies to the power and strength of a core memory, and when we legitimize and celebrate the varied interpretations of a common memory, we are seeing pluralism in action. The precondition for pluralism, of course, is that everyone is familiar with the core memory. First we have to teach the memory, inculcate it, and help people make it their own. As said above, we do that with narratives, retelling them, reenacting them, and making the retelling of collective memories part of the individual memories that we all carry. With that foundation, we are then able to develop our own interpretations of those core memories and make them our own.

Unfortunately, though, what we often see in the Jewish world today is that, as a result of not being familiar with their own family's memories, people choose to live somebody else's memories. They are more familiar with and more connected to the stories and concepts that come from other cultures and religions. This is assimilation. In contrast to that, I am proud to be a Jewish pluralist, which to me means being able to legitimize different interpretations of a common memory; assimilation, on the other hand, is living someone else's memory. I am committed to living and expressing our Jewish memories, even (or especially) when there are different interpretations of those common memories.

Memory is one of the most powerful tools we have to build Jewish Peoplehood. It reappears multiple times in this book, through the stories I tell, the choices I made when educating for Jewish Peoplehood, and my prescriptions for the Jewish future.

# 4

# Judaism is NOT a Religion!
# The Jews are a Family

*In New York City there is a bank. A very
successful bank. It was once called Chase
Manhattan, and they had a slogan that every
kid in New York knew: "You have a friend at
Chase Manhattan." When a well-known Israeli
bank opened up their first branch in New York,
they came up with their own slogan: "You may
have a friend at Chase Manhattan, but we're
mishpochah (family)." To my mind, they hit
the nail on the head. You want to know who
the Jews are? That's who we are – a family!*

I am lucky to have experienced Jewish life in different locations
and especially lucky to have grown up in South Africa. The approach to Jewish life that has emerged from all of these experiences has cemented for me the notion of family as my preferred
way of describing the Jewish People. We are not a religion nor
simply a nationality. Rather, we are an extended family, a tribe
that shares a common past and future, a national home, reli-

gious customs, and a language. In more academic language, we might be referred to as an "ethnos," a group with a collective belief in a common ancestry. I prefer the more accessible language of "family."

Just like every other tribal or ethnic group, the Jewish People maintains its own separateness in a distinctive way; distinctiveness is, in fact, a critical value for us. I see group distinctiveness as positive and essential if we are to respect others, and I learned this growing up in South Africa where, of course, it wasn't always a good thing to be certain kinds of different. I learned about difference when I realized that people were different. In South Africa the primary lesson about difference was based on skin color. I was told to talk more softly when the black servants were in the room. I was told not to talk about politics and human equality in public. I sensed that this could make you a traitor to the society.

I grew up in a non-Jewish suburb of Johannesburg. My neighbors on all sides were white, but I never visited their homes. My friends were the Jewish kids who lived further away and not immediately next door. It was my Jewish friends who were invited to my birthday party, not the kids next door. I was obviously different, but I wasn't really sure how. For us, as for all South Africans at the time, skin color was important, but it wasn't the only marker of difference; I just couldn't quite figure out what the other important factor was. It couldn't be religion; I never went to synagogue, just like my next-door neighbors never went to church. It had to be something ethnic, but I just wasn't sure what it was.

It wasn't until I traveled with my father to Swaziland that I made sense of this paradox. I was a young child, maybe seven or eight, and I went with my father on a trip to Swaziland where he, as the professional leader of the Zionist movement in South Africa, had been invited to meet the King of Swaziland. As a senior community leader, my father was often introduced to important people, and his driver, Daniel, who was related to the Swazi royal family, had made the introduction. When we arrived at the chief's compound, I remember my father being introduced: "Chief of the Swazis meet the Chief of the Jews." Of course, my father wasn't exactly the Chief of the Jews, but he was a very important Jew, and I instinctively understood that this introduction was appropriate. It also conveyed the essence of an idea that made profound sense and has impacted my thinking about Jews and Judaism to this day – namely, that Jews are basically a tribe.

The notion of tribe isn't used much today to talk about Judaism; the term has fallen out of favor, perhaps because of the negative connotations attached to "tribalism." Jews don't want to be thought of as self-centered, closed-minded, or parochial. But for a South African child in the 1950s, the notion of tribe was extremely familiar and quite positive. I knew what tribes were; in South Africa everyone defined themselves first and foremost as a member of a particular tribe. There were white tribes – the Dutch settlers, British ex-pats, and Jews (among others); there were the Coloureds – people with mixed race ancestry; and then, of course, there were many black tribes often with passionate rivalries between them. Each tribe had its own language, religion, culture, and customs. People lived in tribal communities, and their first loyalty was to other members of their group. Even today in South Africa, the post-apartheid "rainbow nation" remains divided into these groupings which continue to define belonging. People want to retain their tribalism despite the occasional disadvantages. So, when I first heard Jews being referred to as a tribe, it was clear to me that this, indeed, is what we are.

A tribe is essentially an extended family, and today when I talk and teach about the Jewish People, I focus on the notion of family. The metaphor of family is a core idea for understanding the collective identity of the Jews: we are a diverse, multifaceted family with many different branches, who, nevertheless, remain linked in a deep and fundamental way. Not only do we call ourselves family – *bnei yisrael* (the children – literally "the sons and daughters" – of Israel) – but the Torah also refers to us that way, choosing not to call us "Jews" or "Hebrews" but to focus on the familial link. Indeed, the first book of the Bible is nothing if not the story of this family and its formation.

We all have our roots in our own smaller, more intimate families, as the children of one set of parents with siblings or cousins with whom we share memories and experiences. And, just like the Jewish People, we expand our families as we grow, and our sense of belonging broadens to include other more distant family members, who make up the tribe as a whole.

Being a family and seeing ourselves as a family is a way of explaining the connection that Jews feel for each other; the ties of empathy and sympathy and even of irritation and anger. It reflects a reality in which we can both love each other and argue with each other at the same time. The capacity to love someone you have never met and truly care about their welfare can only be explained by the notion of family. Caring enough to argue with someone you don't really know is similarly indicative of a strong relationship. If we didn't care about that person, we wouldn't bother engaging with them, but when we care enough to get involved, even to argue, it reflects a bond between us. It is that very combination of loving and arguing that constitutes family.

This point is illustrated by an experience I once had when visiting a friend who was sitting *shiva*, the week-long period of mourning for a close relative. When I got to his home, his five-year-old daughter, whom I had never met before, saw me come in, turned to her father, and said, "Daddy, who is this and do I love him?" She was, in other words, asking: Is he one of us? Is he one of my family?

## Family Membership

The most common and obvious way to join the family is to be born into it, a passive act about which we have no choice. However, taking an active role in the family does demand sustained involvement and effort. We may inherit our relatives automatically, but it isn't until we deliberately create ties with them that they become our family in the deepest sense. And creating family ties requires communication, the cultivation of shared experiences, and, most importantly, the connecting of our own individual memories to the collective memories of the extended family.

Of course, there are also those who choose to join the family, to bind their future to the future of a people with whom they had no initial ties. In the world today we know that more and more Jews are going to marry non-Jews. How we relate to this question is central to the future of the Jewish People and remains a controversial issue. I believe that we have to welcome these people into the family and take advantage of this opportunity for the Jewish People. After all, how many times in history have we had non-Jews loving us enough to want to actually join us? At the same time, if someone wants to join a small Jewish family by marrying one of its members, they must also engage with the serious prospect that they are, in fact, joining the bigger, extended Jewish family. The next logical question concerns the conditions for entering the big Jewish family. What do we want these new Jews to commit to? How do they join the family in the family home?

I recognize that, in the Jewish world of today, intermarriage is considered highly problematic because of the risk of assimilation. Indeed, it reflects the fact that Jews have already assimilated into the majority cultures in which they live. I do not believe assimilation is a good thing; I am committed to the continued significant renaissance of Jewish life and the Jewish People. However, I make an important distinction between intermarriage and assimilation. Intermarriage does not necessarily have to mean assimilation. Even though this approach is challenged by our historical experience, things are different today; at no previous time has intermarriage been a fact of life like it is today. I believe it is critical to help those who are married to Jews understand what it means to join the family, formally or not, and how they can make decisions so that their children will have Jewish memories and be active members of the family in the future. What's more, I believe we have to think about welcoming those who choose to live with a member of our family even if they haven't (or won't) become a full member of the family. Can we think creatively about these possibilities?

## The Book of Ruth

In Jewish tradition, the biblical character Ruth serves as a model of a non-Jew joining the Jewish family. The words Ruth uses when she tells her mother-in-law, Naomi, that she is not returning to Moab to her people are the words that, even today, new Jews declare during their conversion process: "Your people is my people, your God is my God" (Ruth 1:16). The order of these phrases is significant. First, Ruth accepts that she is joining a new people, taking on the rights and responsibilities of being part of the Jewish family. Only then does she pledge her allegiance to the monotheistic Jewish deity. If a person wants to join another religion, such as Christianity, it is sufficient to say, "Your God is my God"; but Judaism is different. It isn't primarily a religion. It is an ethnic group, a people, a civilization with a God-centered culture, and Ruth's words express that idea.

## Adoption Not Conversion

In order to welcome new Jews into the family, I strongly believe that their choice should be referred to as "adoption" and not "conversion." The Hebrew verb meaning to convert to Judaism is *le'hit'gayer*, which is the reflexive form of the root *la'gur*, to live with. This reflects the idea that when a person joins the Jewish family, they don't suddenly become a new person or change their very being; rather they move in with the family. Instead of calling these people "converts," we should – and I will hereafter – call them "adopted Jews" or "new Jews."

It should be noted that there is a concept of a "converted Jew" (*yehudi mumar*) in Jewish tradition, but it refers to Jews who join another religion. Even though these individuals probably considered themselves Christians or Muslims, the rabbis still considered them Jews. In Tractate Sanhedrin 44a the Talmud teaches that "even though a Jew has sinned, he [or she] is still a Jew." In other words, no matter what a person does, even if they try to leave the family, it doesn't change the essence of who they are.

## Maimonides' Letter to Obadiah the Convert

Just as we don't want a child who was adopted to feel that they don't belong, so too in the case of those who choose to become Jewish. We are told in Midrash Tanhuma (Vayera 14) that it is forbidden to keep reminding new Jews that they are converts, because once they have changed their status, they are just Jews, full and equal members of the family. The essence of the adoption process is the slow cultivation of the family's collective memories, and therefore prospective Jews participate in the rituals of the extended family, learn the stories that the family tells, and start to speak of themselves as "we." At the end of the process an "adoption ceremony" of sorts takes place. The new Jew chooses a new name, taking on a new public identity as a member of the tribe. The men are considered to be the "son of Abraham" and the women either the "daughter of Sarah" or the "daughter of Ruth." This new parentage is a sign of their adoption into the Jewish People. These new parents do not, of course, replace their biological parents either emotionally or according to Jewish law, but they are nevertheless viewed metaphorically as an additional set of parents to be added to the individual's genealogy and memory.

A striking example of this principle and the result of the adoption process can be found in a famous twelfth-century letter written by Maimonides, known as "The Letter of Maimonides to Obadiah the Convert." In this letter, Maimonides replies to the question posed by Obadiah who asks whether, as a "convert," he is permitted to say various prayers and blessings that are factually untrue in his case, including "Our God and God of our forefathers," "who has sanctified us by his commandments," and "You have taken us out of the land of Egypt." Maimonides replies unequivocally that "converts" should say all these prayers. It isn't important whether a person can trace their genealogy back to the Bible; what matters is that they have joined the family and become part of the sociological process of gaining the collective Jewish memories of that family. Maimonides' approach is universally accepted today. It reflects the understanding that the collective identity of the Jews began with Abraham, to whom we refer as *Avraham Avinu*, "Abraham our Father." This reminds us of our identity as a family and connects us, metaphorically and spiritually, to these beginnings.

## Connections

As mentioned above, building connections with members of the Jewish family is a critical and ongoing process that is necessary for the continuity of the family. It requires us to be active members, engaged with the family in many different ways: for example, participating and being involved in shared family memories (such as those described in Chapter 3) or sharing a language, a covenant, and a relationship with Israel (to be described in the following chapters). The role of Jewish education is to use these levers to help individuals connect their own individual memories to the collective memories of the Jewish People.

## Judaism Is Not a Religion

The concept of Jews as an extended family is unfamiliar to many Jews who relate to Judaism primarily in religious terms. My point that Judaism is not a religion is particularly challenging for American Jews, as I discovered on my first visit to America.

It was 1967, a few months after the Six Day War, and I had newly arrived in Baltimore, Maryland. As I was driving down the New Jersey Turnpike I saw a large billboard proclaiming: "Families that Pray Together, Stay Together." It was signed by the Council of Protestants, Catholics, and Jews. What was going on here? I was so stunned that I almost drove my car off the road! Protestants and Catholics are indeed religious groups. But Jews? Jews are not a religious group, and they don't belong in a group with Protestants and Catholics.

When I arrived in Baltimore, I discovered that there was a party to welcome the new *shaliach* to town. Seeing that I was the *shaliach*, I went to the party. I was introduced to the executive director of the Jewish Federation. I said, "Bob, fix that sign. Judaism is not a religion!" He looked shocked; he had no idea what I was talking about. I continued: "Judaism is not a religion! I know because my father told me so." Bob claimed that his father had taught him the very opposite! The conversation went on: "Bob, do you keep kosher?" "Only if there is nothing else!" he replied. "Do you keep Shabbat?" "No." "Do you go to synagogue?" "Once or twice a year to see the guys." "What is

Judaism?" I asked. "A religion," he replied. "Are you religious?" "No!" What are you then?" "I am Jewish!" He could have asked me the same questions. "Do you keep kosher?" "All the time," is my answer. "Do you keep Shabbat?" "At least once a week!" "Do you ever pray?" "Three times a day." And to the question, "Is Judaism a religion?" I would still have answered, "No." "What are you then?" "I am Jewish!"

This experience shocked me then and continues to shock me today whenever I encounter Jews who think that they belong to a religion. It happens all the time, both in Israel and in the wider Jewish world, and it is a distortion of who and what we are.

A couple of years ago I got a phone call from a rabbi, the head of a local religious council. He was very angry with me: "I have to take issue with you. Some American students were at my house on Friday night and they told me that you are teaching that Judaism is not a religion! How dare you say something like that! You are ruining generations of young people." I thanked him politely for his opinion and took the opportunity to ask him a question of Jewish law. "I have a non-Jewish neighbor who sees me putting on *tefillin* every day when I am praying on the balcony. He wants to learn how to put on *tefillin* and asked me to go and help him buy some and put them on. Can I help him do that?" As predicted, the rabbi burst out, "Absolutely not. Under no circumstances can you help him do it!" "But Rabbi, why?" I asked. "Because he is not a member of the Jewish People" was his answer. Then he stuttered a little and said, "Ah, perhaps you are right. Maybe Judaism isn't just a religion. I never thought of that. I will think about it and get back to you." I never heard from him again.

If we Jews really were a religious group, wouldn't we want to spread our religious teachings, just like other religions do? After all, a religion is understood as the truth of all truths, and religions want others to accept those truths. If we had that approach, we would actively look for those non-Jews who wanted to try on *tefillin* and perform other *mitzvot*. We certainly wouldn't say it was forbidden for them to participate, because we would be hoping they would join us. But we are not a religion, we are a people, and our rituals and values apply only to those who are members of our People. There is no inherent value for us in expanding our membership, because we believe that all other peoples have their own unique role in the world; they don't have to be like us.

## The Global Jewish Family

We live in a global world today, but the Jewish People has always been a global people, and despite the varying sizes of the different communities, I believe that they are all valuable. My intention has always been to encourage all Jews, wherever they live, to see themselves as valuable contributors to the whole Jewish People. Everyone in the family can make a contribution to the whole, and we are all equally responsible for one another. Yet, often, Jews in different countries have different ways of relating to their Jewishness and being part of the family.

As president of the global Hillel movement I saw this firsthand. One time I went to open the Hillel in Buenos Aires, Argentina. I was the guest speaker, and as I can't speak a word of Spanish, they sent me a translator. She didn't know English, but she knew Hebrew. So I started my lecture in Hebrew and found the audience laughing even before she translated my jokes. To my great surprise, they had understood! When I asked how many of them understood Hebrew, the vast majority raised their hands. When I asked how many of them could recite the *Shema* (the central statement of Jewish faith which is traditionally recited daily), many fewer raised their hands. In America it would be the exact opposite; they would know the *Shema* from Hebrew School but would certainly not understand my Hebrew lecture!

I often ask Jews from different backgrounds to help me understand their approach to being Jewish by suggesting categories that are comparable to "Jewish." I use a chart with three columns. Each column contains objects or concepts that go together – for example, "apples, oranges, bananas," or "shirts, jackets, pants." Then I write "Jew" and ask my audience to fill in the blanks. What is to "Jew" as orange is to apple? American Jews almost always fill in the blanks with other religions – i.e., Protestants, Catholics, Muslims. Israeli Jews always include Arabs in the list, because for them Arabs are their significant other. Russian-speaking Jews always include Russian as a category, followed by something like Georgian, indicating that, for them, Judaism is an ethnic and cultural category, not a religious one, and that they don't define themselves as Russian. Latin Americans are the least predictable and usually claim, perhaps correctly, that there is nothing comparable.

For additional proof of the different ways in which Jews from different countries understand being Jewish, just look at the ways that Jews in the Former Soviet Union (FSU) express their Judaism compared to the ways that American Jews do. Jews from the FSU tend to express their Judaism in cultural ways, such as learning Hebrew or Yiddish and engaging with literature and culture, whereas North American Jews tend to express their Jewishness through religious forms. Nonetheless, they share a sense of belonging to something, and this binds them together. Indeed, Jews all over the world cared enough to help free Soviet Jews from communist oppression, and both Russian-speaking and North American Jews arrive in Israel and feel at home in similar ways, even though they come from different Jewish cultures.

## Being Distinctively Jewish and Universally Human

One of the challenges in the Jewish world is the weakening of the collective bonds that Jews feel for other Jews. The notion of a tribe is hard to reconcile with universal values; for many, it feels overly exclusive or restrictive. Yet this tension between the universal and the particular has been present in our tradition for hundreds (if not thousands) of years, as can be seen in two different pieces of exegesis from our most authoritative commentators, Rashi and Maimonides. The medieval commentator Rashi starts his famous commentary on the Torah by noting that it begins with God creating the world: "In the beginning, God created the heaven and the earth." Rashi questions why the Torah starts this way. Surely if the Torah is for the Jewish People, it should start with the first commandment God gives them as a People? In answer, Rashi explains that the first verse of the Torah comes to teach that the whole world belongs to God, and therefore He can decide who He is giving the Land of Israel to – namely, the Jewish People. For Rashi, the Torah has a particularistic stance, focusing on the distinctiveness of the Jews and their Land, even from the first verse. Maimonides expresses a more universalistic position when he interprets the famous Mishnaic teaching from the second century CE that "anyone who destroys (or saves) the life of a Jew, it is as if he has destroyed (or saved) an entire world" (Tractate Sanhedrin 4:5). Maimonides rewrote this principle by leaving out the word "Jew"; for him, anyone who destroys any human life is guilty of destroying the whole world. He thus emphasized the universal, the idea that all human beings (and not just Jews) are born equal in the image of God.

Both Rashi and Maimonides suggest how I have to be Jewish; Rashi teaches me what it means to be part of a particular group, while Maimonides teaches me that we are all part of the human race and share qualities with every human being. The Jewish family lives in the tension between both of these approaches.

I too live in perpetual tension between my universal and particular tendencies. I am both Avraham Infeld the Jew and Avraham Infeld the human being. Sometimes one of these identities is primary; sometimes the other takes over. However, I aspire to live with both simultaneously and to make them whole. There is never a time when I am only one or the other. I am always both, even when they are in conflict and there is tension between them. To be a member of the extended Jewish family in the twenty-first century is to be universally human and distinctively Jewish at the same time. It is also to connect through shared memories with other Jews, even those who appear to be distant relatives, and to turn that belonging into behaviors that will contribute both to the continued significant renaissance of the Jewish People and the improving of the world.

# 5

# God, Mount Sinai, and Being Right

*Every Friday night my father would make
Kiddush for our family. Yet, as I have
already mentioned, he wasn't an observant
Jew and was proud to say, "I am an atheist,*
Baruch Hashem *(Thank God)." One week
I interrupted him and asked him why he was
making Kiddush if God didn't exist. "You are
right," he said, "but I am a member of the
Jewish People, and I am doing what Jews all
over the world are doing. I may be an atheist,
but I am still a Jew!"*

If, as I said in the previous chapter, the Jewish People is not
a religion, why does God appear here at all? It doesn't make
sense! Surely, if we are talking about God, we must be a religion? Yet, I believe that God is a critical part of this story
because He (or She) is a core component of the culture of the
Jewish People. I admit that this may be counter-intuitive – we
have been influenced by other religions and so it is not the
typical way we talk about or relate to God. For this reason, I
found this chapter the most difficult to write; yet it is also one

of the most important, because it truly reflects my approach to Jewish Peoplehood. I believe that God is a central part of the Jewish People's experience and that God, for us, is primarily a collective and not an individual experience. The Jewish People's culture is a God-centered culture.

As I have already described, a core memory of the Jewish People is the memory of Mount Sinai. On our journey from Egypt to the Land of Israel we stopped in the desert and something happened there, not to us as individuals but as a collective. And through that collective experience with God we became a People. Out of that connection to God emerges the covenant – namely, the special relationship between the Jewish People and God. This is a relationship in three parts: first, we testify to the existence of God; second, God gives us a role in the development of our culture and traditions; and third, we recognize that God did not create a perfect world and therefore it is our responsibility to be God's partner in perfecting it.

## Humans Are Not God

The relationship between human beings and God is, first and foremost, the understanding that we are not God, we are only human beings, and as such we are limited and cannot be all-powerful. We have a tendency to believe that we are enormously powerful: even Pharaoh and the Egyptians couldn't stop us. The experience of Mount Sinai comes as a humbling reminder of the limits of our control. The first of the Ten Commandments states: "I am the Lord your God." But that isn't actually a commandment. Rather, it is a reminder of our obligation to testify to the existence of God. This is both reassuring and cautionary: God is telling us not to worry that others will control us and promising to always look after us, but, at the same time, He is warning us not to assume His role because that job is already taken! In championing this idea, the Jewish

People are playing an educational role by teaching the world that there is a God. This is hugely important; there is nothing more dangerous than a world in which human beings think they are God.

## The Written and Oral Torahs

I remember learning Talmud with my father when I was seven years old. We read the *midrash* that talks about both the written and oral Torah being given at Mount Sinai. I asked my father, "How long would it have taken God to write the oral Torah? Surely He could have written it down if He wanted to? Why did he leave it oral?" My father got up, walked around the table to where I was sitting, picked me up, and gave me a huge hug and kiss. "Never ever forget that question," he said to me, "that is the most important question you will ever ask about being Jewish."

According to Jewish tradition, the Jewish People received two Torahs at Mount Sinai: the written Torah (the text we call the Five Books of Moses) and the oral Torah (the oral teachings that explain and interpret the written Torah). While the written text of the Torah is fixed and cannot be changed, the oral interpretations are more fluid. They are debated, interpreted, and added to by Jews throughout the generations, and by interpreting them, we work together with God to create the truth that is right for the Jewish People at any given time. The oral Torah evolved over centuries into the rabbinic literature of the Mishnah and the Talmud. It was eventually written down, but it didn't start that way and, according to many rabbinic opinions, it was never meant to be that way. My father believed the story that the oral Torah was given in oral form in order to enable the Jewish People to be in an ongoing partnership with God and thus create Jewish culture. According to my father, when Rabbi Yehuda HaNasi oversaw the compilation of the oral Torah around the year 200 CE, this was perhaps essential, but it has turned out to have the serious and unfortunate result of the Torah becoming fixed and barely evolving.

Despite the fact that the oral Torah has been written down, we remain, I believe, in partnership with God, a partnership that actually enables holiness. We see this in many examples. Why is it that if you eat a small piece of bread, the traditional Grace after Meals goes on for many pages, but if you eat a truck full of oranges, it is just one short sentence? As I learned from Rabbi Kenneth Brander at Yeshiva University, this doesn't appear logical, unless you understand that God's partnership with the Jewish People brings holiness into the world. When God performs unilateral acts, like giving the Torah at Mount Sinai or creating the world, there is no inherent holiness. No one even knows where Mount Sinai is; it is not an important place in Jewish tradition. Rather, holiness is created when human beings and God are in partnership together: building the Temple, making bread, celebrating holidays, and repairing the world (*Tikkun Olam*). These are the times that we sanctify and the acts to which we ascribe holiness. In many instances we say blessings to recognize holiness, and so for the fruit of a tree in which we had minimal input – even if it is a truck full of oranges – the blessing is short and simple. For a piece of bread, however, significant human action was required in partnership with that of God, and therefore the blessing is long and raises the experience of making and eating bread to the highest level of holiness.

The covenant reflects our belief that we have a partnership with God where we interpret and implement the values and the rituals of the Torah. Those values and rituals, which traditionally are expressed as commandments (*mitzvot*), improve our communities and remind us who we are. The rituals face inward, connecting us with each other and reminding us that we are all part of the extended family, while values face outward, giving us the power and the energy to help make the world a better place. Personally, I love the idea of God who was present at the start of our collective history, gave us the tools we need, and then left things in our hands.

## Perfecting the World (*Tikkun Olam*)

Thus, beyond the Jewish People's role in partnership with God for the benefit of our own People, our relationship with God also requires us to take responsibility to improve the world for the benefit of humanity. This stems from the recognition that God did not create a perfect world and that we are required to be a partner with God in perfecting it. This is the root of our obligation to *Tikkun Olam*.

## You Don't Have to Be Me to Be Right!

Each people has its unique purpose, a way in which its distinctiveness can add something to the world. As I have already said, for me, the Jewish People's uniqueness is based on our responsibility to testify to the existence of God and to introduce the teachings of the Torah with its core values of justice to the world. The Jewish People, our family, has a particular set of commandments. We call them the 613 *mitzvot*, and they are our birthright. According to tradition, to be a fully righteous Jew, you are bound by all the *mitzvot*; that is what is right for us and reflects our particular covenant with God. However, non-Jews, we are told, have a different set of *mitzvot*, the Seven Noachide Laws, and that is what is right for them. The message of the Jewish People to other peoples is, therefore, that what is right for us – keeping 613 *mitzvot* – is not a universal value, and that being righteous does not require universal standards of behavior or belief. We say to the world, "You don't have to be me to be right!" This statement is a profound and critical lesson. It runs counter to all totalitarian ideologies, from Hitler and Stalin to ISIS and radical Christianity. All fundamentalists are driven by the basic principle that the only way to be right is to be just like them. Judaism, on the other hand, teaches the opposite: you don't have to be me to be right.

We are not, however, afraid to claim that there is a right approach. It's just that we believe that there is more than one right, and so we can create space both for what is right for us and what is right for others. The role of the Jewish People is, therefore, to demonstrate by our very existence and our particular connection to Torah that there are more than one rights in the world.

## God and the Collective

As I have explained here, I believe that a collective relationship with God, whether or not He actually exists, is a core component of Jewish Peoplehood. You cannot attach yourself to the God of Israel without attaching yourself also to the People of Israel. It is through belonging to the Jewish People and being part of the collective memories and expressions of Jewish life that we have our unique relationship with God. For example, just think about the *mitzvot* of the holiday of Sukkot. We shake the *lulav* (palm branches) and *etrog* (citron) and some other branches for eight days, a spectacle which is surely strange (at the very least!). For me, commandments like this are not religious acts and I doubt whether God cares about the details. They are primarily an expression of distinctiveness; they evoke the collective memory of living in rickety huts in the desert and remind us of who we are on a regular basis, tying us to our culture and our People. I imagine God laughing at us indulgently every year as we build our *sukkot* and shake our *lulavim*.

## My Personal God

In this chapter I have tried to show why I believe that God is a crucial component of Jewish Peoplehood. At the same time I do also have a personal relationship with God. I believe there is a deep human need for spiritual connection and that individuals find that spiritual connection in multiple ways. But those are individual stories, not collective ones, and they have relevance only for that individual. My own personal relationship with God is not always clear. While I don't know for sure whether God exists, I choose to live in a world in which He is very present, and I come close to Him through the particular Jewish prism I have inherited. So I therefore choose to go to synagogue every morning, put on *tefillin*, and learn Talmud every day, and through these things I connect myself simultaneously to the Jewish People and the universal God.

# 6

# Hebrew:
# The Language of the Jewish People

*When I was a child, my father would periodically look at my books to see what I was learning in school. Once he noticed that my Hebrew teacher was teaching us the past, present, and future tenses. My Hebrew teacher was my mother. My father looked at my book and asked in surprise, "Who taught you this nonsense?" "Your wife!" I answered. "This isn't right," my father insisted. "There is no present tense in the Hebrew language. In English you can say, 'I swim, I run, I talk, I walk.' But in Hebrew you can't do that. All you can say is, 'I am swimming, I am running.' In Hebrew the present is always moving, it doesn't exist on its own; it exists to connect the past to the future. That is the purpose of the present."*

## Language and the Transmission of Culture

Language is not only a method of communication. It is also a method for transferring culture from generation to generation. There can be no continuation of culture without language. That is why Hebrew is such an important part of what it means to be Jewish. As my friend Leon Wieseltier said so eloquently in his essay "Language, Identity, and the Scandal of American Jewry":

> Our language is our incommensurable inflection of our humanity; our unique way of presenting, not least to ourselves, what our unique way is through the world. Our language is our element; our beginning; our air; the air peculiar to us. Even our universalism comes to us (like everybody else's universalism) in a particular language.

The particular language I grew up with was, indeed, Hebrew. It was an important part of my life as a child, and my parents spoke to each other and to me primarily in Hebrew, even though they also spoke Polish, Russian, Yiddish, and German as well as English. I can now distinguish the moments that my parents used a particular language. "Eat your food" or "close the door" were said in English; "I love you" or "why are you doing that?" were in Hebrew. Moments of rebuke and affection – the important things – were delivered in Hebrew, while logistical or technical instructions were in English. My father spoke very formal Hebrew. He never said *"Ani Rotzeh"*; rather the more formal *"Ani Hafetz,"* that Israelis made fun of. My mother was a Hebrew teacher, and even though her first language was not Hebrew, she brought me up with the songs and stories of native-born Israeli children with Hebrew as their mother tongue. My parents' conscious decision to prioritize Hebrew, when they could have spoken to each other in any of several languages, was their way of participating in Jewish culture by using the language of Jewish culture. I, consequently, grew up feeling that all other languages that Jews have spoken are passing phases.

I also internalized the fact that languages define tribal identity, because it was not only English and Hebrew that were spoken in our house but also African tribal languages. It was usually Xhosa, but when Enos came to work for us, he was from a different tribe and didn't speak Xhosa. The cook didn't know his language, Ndebele, so they had to speak English between themselves. I learned from this that every tribe is distinct in its language.

One of my earliest memories evokes a confusion around Hebrew, when it became clear to me that not all Jews were like us. It was 1949, and I was six years old. A man from a kibbutz with a long, flowing white beard wearing shorts and sandals – it was summer in Israel, and the fact that it was winter in South Africa made no difference to him – came to South Africa. His name was Zerubavel, and to me, he was like a character from a movie or perhaps a prophet. He was one of the heads of the Israeli political party Mapam, and he had come to South Africa to raise money for the upcoming elections. My father organized a meeting of various members of the Jewish community in our home. I remember sitting on my father's lap, and Zerubavel started to speak in Yiddish, as he didn't speak English. My father interrupted him forcefully, saying "Zerubavel, talk as a Jew. Speak Hebrew and I will translate. Yiddish has no place in this house. We already have a state." I remember being startled by my father's insistence that everyone should speak a language that was probably the least comfortable language for the assembled group. Why was Hebrew so important?

Once a month, my parents would have a group of their

friends come over for a Hebrew evening. Someone played the piano, and I would lie in bed listening to them singing Hebrew songs. Later, someone would give a talk in Hebrew. But they all speak English! These are the parents of my friends. I know them, and they all talk English, so why are they speaking Hebrew? My confusion deepened when it became clear that my parents were talking to me in a language that all the kids in school hated learning and that no other families spoke at home.

What I came to understand through my parents' insistence on Hebrew is that Hebrew is an integral part of what makes Jews distinct. We see this in a little-known story in the Torah where Jacob and his father-in-law, Laban, who have had some conflict between them, are preparing to part ways peacefully. Jacob is taking his wives and children back to Israel, and as part of their covenant of separation, they build a pile of stones as a physical monument to their agreement: "And Jacob called it *Gal-ed*; Laban called it *Yagar-Saharduta*" (Genesis 31:47). These two names mean the same thing, "a testimonial pile of stones," but in two different languages. So, as these two men separate into their distinctive tribes, they each take care to use their own language to name what is important to them. That is what we do all the time as Jews: we name things and refer to our values using our own particular language, and thus we become and remain distinctive.

## Hebrew and Jewish Values

There are many examples in Hebrew of how our cultural values are carried by the language. One of my favorites is the word "*le'hitahev*," which is translated as "falling in love." Where does the idea of "falling in love" come from? What does that phrase communicate? In English it comes from the Christian idea that Adam committed the first sin when he ate the fruit in the Garden of Eden. When he committed this crime, driven by passion, he was falling in love. In this culture, love becomes a sign of a human failing, a falling into sin. In Hebrew, however, we reject this approach and understand something totally different. "*Le'hitahev*" means "to love" but in a reflexive form. In other words, being in love is always mutual, it includes both sides, and is both active and passive at the same time. The word carries the understanding that the more you give in love, the more you gain. It is very far from the notion of sin or failure.

Another example of the transmission of our cultural values through language can be seen in the distinction between the word "charity" in English and "*tzedakah*" in Hebrew. Charity comes from the Greek word "*caritas*," which implies a compassion for the suffering of others. Jews, however, do not do charity; we do *tzedakah*, which comes from the Hebrew word "*tzedek*" meaning justice and reflects our responsibility to take action. While charity begins with the suffering of the other, *tzedakah* begins with our personal responsibility to help others.

## Hebrew and the Zionist Revolution

It is often said that the Zionist movement brought a dead language back to life. That is not strictly true. After all, Jewish literature throughout the ages was always written in Hebrew. The difference was that Hebrew wasn't a spoken language used for everyday life, it was used mainly for liturgy, education, and literature. When they wanted to speak, Jews spoke the languages of the surrounding culture, and at the same time they developed the hybrid Jewish languages of the Diaspora. When they tried to speak German, it came out as Yiddish. When they tried to speak Spanish, it came out as Ladino. The exception to this is English. When Jews in America started to speak English, they became fluent and, as Leon Wieseltier claimed in the previously quoted essay, they have become illiterate in

Hebrew, which, he predicts, will have disastrous consequences for their connection to Jewish culture and the Jewish People.

The Zionist revolution was, therefore, responsible for making Hebrew an everyday spoken language that could evolve with the ongoing needs of society and help to create culture. This was unprecedented in linguistic history. Today, the Academy of the Hebrew Language continues to create Hebrew words for new inventions and ideas, and Hebrew remains a vehicle for Jewish culture of the past and the future.

# 7

# The Land of Israel: The Indigenous Home of the Jewish People

*As a child in South Africa, I remember asking my father to explain why we prayed for rain in the summer. It was December, and in synagogue the prayers included a request for rain, which no child in South Africa wants at that time of year! My father's answer was very straightforward: "Our rain doesn't fall in South Africa, it falls in Israel!" Try to grow up normal with an answer like that! But being Jewish is not being normal. Being Jewish means living with the knowledge that, irrespective of where you actually live, it is only in the Land of Israel that the Jewish People are indigenous. With the lesson of the rain my father taught me about the deep connection between the Jewish People and the Land of Israel. As individuals, we can pray for rain in South Africa, or wherever else we may live, but the Jewish People's collective rain falls in Israel.*

## The Land of Israel

As the eternal destination of the Jewish People, the Land of Israel is and was critical to our formation as a People; it is the land we were promised at birth, the repository of many of our collective memories, and the one place in the world where the whole Jewish People has a home, even if they don't use it. It is the only place in the world where the Jewish People are indigenous. The connection to the Land of Israel is commemorated regularly (even daily) in Jewish life and culture – in our texts, prayers, and customs: we face the Land of Israel when we pray; we have *mitzvot* that apply only there and ascribe holiness to its produce; Jewish poetry, songs, and art have expressed the relationship of the people to its land for centuries. Together these things have constructed collective memories rooted in this particular place.

## Exile from the Land

The Land of Israel is the place from which the Jewish People were exiled thousands of years ago and to which we waited to return. Our tradition understands that we were exiled because of our sins and that our return to the Land would therefore be understood as God's forgiveness and would herald the Messianic Era. Until the advent of modernity, the Jewish People waited patiently to be forgiven and understood that their golden age was still ahead of them. I believe that nothing contributed more to the longevity of the Jewish People in exile than the dream (and certainty) that one day they would be forgiven and would return to the Land of Israel.

## Zionism

It was therefore not surprising that when Jews in the ghettos of Europe confronted modernity, some of them made a connection between the Land of Israel and their modern nationalist aspirations. They assumed no connection between their new-found nationalist ideology and God's promise to return the Jewish People to their home, but nevertheless, it made sense to them to direct their attention to the Land of Israel. Indeed, the Zionist movement rejected every other alternative offered for the creation of the Jewish State and (despite fiery debate and other options) persevered in its commitment to the Land of Israel. They declared that the national home of the Jewish People must be in the Land of Israel and their anthem, *Hatikva*, invoked the ancient dream of the Jewish People to return to their Land. The color of the Zionist flag was blue and white to evoke the colors of their *tallitot* (prayer shawls). At the same time, the majority of Jews, who responded differently to the challenges of modernity, regarded as blasphemous this preempting of the return to the land without God's express permission and forgiveness.

## Two Master Stories

Within 50 years, however, the Zionist movement achieved its goal of creating a modern, secular national home for the Jewish People in the Land of Israel. This was the successful application of the laws of modern nationalism by the Jewish People, inspired by, but not dependent on the ancient connection to the Land. At this point we can identify two distinctly different master stories of the Jewish People's relationship to the land that have developed and that continue to influence and challenge us today.

The first master story is the traditional story that we have already described: the Jewish People are indigenous to Israel, have an unbreakable and mythical bond with the land, and always maintained a spiritual connection through prayer and ritual, believing that we would return as part of a redemptive process that would culminate in the arrival of the Messiah. It is an eternal supra-national story with enormous power to inspire and drive us to action.

The second master story is the adaptation of the first story to a new reality, and it is a narrative in which the Jewish People mobilized to create a political reality similar to other nation-states, in their native land, the Land of Israel. Accordingly, Theodor Herzl and his successors envisioned a democratic state, part of the family of nations, in which Jewish refugees would find a safe haven, modern institutions would govern, and the Jewish People would be just like other nations. This story has propelled the Jewish People to build a modern economy, to absorb millions of immigrants, and to create a thriving Hebrew culture that competes on the world stage.

## The State of Israel

I was born in the years when the State of Israel was coming into being. With its establishment, the ancient relationship of the People with its Land was transformed and evolved into a relationship between the People and its nation-state. I knew the State of Israel as my home even before I lived there. It was the center of our family aspirations and a core part of our family. My earliest childhood memory is of my father sitting and listening to the big radio in the corner of our living room on November 29, 1947. He was listening to the UN vote for the partition of Palestine, and he was crying uncontrollably. I had no idea what had happened, and I remember asking my mother why my father was crying. "From joy," she said, "from sheer joy."

I made *aliyah* when I was 16. I always tell the story that my father came to me and said, "You're a Jewish youngster. There's a Jewish State: Goodbye!" But I also recall a conversation in which my father came to me and said, "I promised your mother I would get you a car if you stayed in South Africa. But God help you if you say yes!" Despite all the Zionism in our house, my mother wasn't thrilled with my *aliyah*; she would miss me and wanted me closer to home. But for my father there was no question; I was going to Israel, and that is what I did.

I arrived in Israel in 1959 accompanied by my father. He came with me for business reasons and then returned to Johannesburg. I went to Kibbutz Lahav where I had a cousin. I had never been to Israel before. I had never been on a kibbutz before, but many of the *shlichim* in South Africa were from kibbutzim, and I was thrilled to have a kibbutznik in my own family. My cousin showed me around the kibbutz. We came to the pigsty, and I was in total shock! I knew that the relationship between the Jewish People and pigs had never been a great love affair! I couldn't contain my shock and anger. "Amira, why are you raising pigs?" Her response was, "Avraham, it was important to be a Jew in South Africa. But now you have come to Israel you can stop being Jewish!"

This experience affected me deeply. I had come to Israel precisely because I was a Jewish youngster, and we Jews had a state. Surely Israel was the place to be more, not less, Jewish? For me, being Jewish and being a Zionist were almost synonymous, while for Amira the two were separate. This was the first time that I saw how my cousin and many other Zionists believed that the State of Israel had turned the Jewish People into a nation and ended the notion of the Jews as a people. It had erased the traditional connection of the People to the Land and replaced it with the connection of citizens to their nation-state. This was highly confusing to me, as I believed then (and still do) that the State of Israel isn't the end of the Jewish People but a new vehicle to ensure the future of the Jewish People.

# The State of Israel:
## The National Home of the Jewish People

According to my conception of Zionism and Israel, the State of Israel is a unique and unusual expression of modern nationalism. While it owes its political roots to the national movements that spread through Europe in the nineteenth century, it is not the same as them. The Zionist movement didn't create a nation-state for a group that physically shared a common geographic area, but rather for the global Jewish People living scattered around the world. For many Zionists the ultimate goal was to turn the People into a nation by having them all move to Israel. This was the Zionism my cousin Amira subscribed to. However, for others, myself included, the People is the essence, and they brought the state into being by applying the laws of modern nationalism to their own unique situation. They didn't intend to replace their cultural, ethnic, and religious identity with a national identity. Rather, they were looking to add national expression to their existing identities in their ancestral homeland. As a result, Israel belongs to all Jews, wherever they are in the world.

This is a fundamentally different conception of a Jewish State than many young Diaspora Jews today expect or understand. Because they see Judaism primarily as a religion, they see Israel as the state established for and by the religion of Judaism. But this is mistaken. The fundamental reason why we have a Jewish State is because we are a People. The Zionist movement that established the State of Israel intended to create a secular state, the state of the Jewish People, not a religious state. And peoples need states in order to survive and thrive. At least in the modern and post-modern world, I believe it is necessary for the survival of all peoples to have a national home where they can be sovereign. That is what Israel is for the Jewish People, and that is why the State of Israel is crucial for the continued significant renaissance of the Jewish People as a whole.

## No More Refugees

When I was born, the noun that most commonly accompanied the adjective "Jewish" was "refugee." There were Jewish refugees everywhere. As we look around the world today, the issue of refugees and displaced persons is undoubtedly one of the biggest global issues. People are moving from Africa, Asia, and the Middle East, and they have nowhere to go. There are more displaced people than at any time in history. At the same time, there isn't a single Jewish refugee. There is only one reason for that: the State of Israel. The Jewish People are not part of the current refugee crisis, because we created a state to ensure our own safety and security.

The creation of the State of Israel turned the entire Jewish People from a family of refugees into a family that would never be refugees again. If, in the past, it was perhaps clearer to more Jews why Israel was so critical to the future well-being of the Jewish People, today it is up to us educators and leaders to articulate more explicitly why the State of Israel is important for all Jews and how it can offer Jews something to share and be proud of. Ending the Jewish refugee problem is a phenomenal achievement which we must appreciate and take pride in. It brings tears to my eyes when I think about it, and we mustn't take it for granted.

## Writing the Next Chapters

When I told my father what my cousin Amira had said to me at Kibbutz Lahav, he also disagreed with her understanding of Zionism. "The purpose of this place," he said, "is that here we will write the 11th, 12th, and 13th chapter of the Jewish story. We are not becoming something new." From this I understood that rather than wiping out Jewish Peoplehood and replacing it with secular nationalism, the State of Israel was enriching Jewish life, providing an additional way to express belonging to the

Jewish People. Yet, I often meet Jews who don't share this approach. Either they believe that we are writing new chapters of the Jewish story without reference to what came before, or they see the first ten chapters as closed and believe there is nothing more to write. My father taught me to take a broader position, which gives the State of Israel profound meaning and purpose. That purpose is not, in my opinion, a rewriting of the whole book but of additional chapters in the book that the Jewish People have been writing and reading for centuries and will, I hope, keep on writing and reading in the future.

# 8

## The State of Israel: A Balancing Act

*My mentor Rabbi David Hartman often
said that if the Jewish People had wanted
to create a normal nation-state like Italy or
Germany, they should have taken up the
offer of Uganda. Their insistence on the
Land of Israel, he claimed, was reminiscent
of a furious adolescent revolting against their
parents, packing their bag, slinging it over their
shoulder, going to the door, slamming it in
fury, and then staying inside!*

*The conscious and somewhat paradoxical
decision to commit to the Land of Israel
opened a Pandora's box of future issues and
compromises that would ensure that the
modern State of Israel could never fit into easy
categories. The result is ongoing societal debates
that deal with core issues of what it means to be
a Jewish state and that break into positions that
are often highly-charged and dichotomous. My
approach is usually to recognize both positions
as fundamentally legitimate and to look for
ways to hold them in constructive tension.
Participating in this national balancing act can
be exhilarating and productive but, at the same*

*time, sometimes frustrating and full of conflict.
This chapter explores some of the constant and
complex balancing acts that ensure that the
State of Israel can both fulfill its purpose for the
Jewish People and be of consequence to as large
a segment of the Jewish People as possible.*

---

## Balancing the Stories in the
## Declaration of Independence

As I have already described, modern Zionism took the traditional master story of the Jewish People and its land and adapted it to create a second narrative in which the Land of Israel
became the place where the people would apply the laws of
modern nationalism to build a secular state. The creative word-
ing of the Declaration of Independence is a masterful example
of this move designed by the leaders of the Zionist movement
who were conscious of the fact that some of the Jews arriving
in the nascent state had experienced modern nationalism and
dreamt of a modern secular homeland, while others saw Israel
in biblical and messianic terms. The writers of the Declaration
of Independence were interested in ensuring that the Declaration have as wide appeal as possible, so they skillfully com-
bined both master stories.

*The Parallel Language of the Declaration of Independence
(see Appendix A for the full text)*

The Declaration starts by asserting the Jewish People's connection to the land and their intention to return: "The people kept
faith with it [the Land of Israel] throughout their Dispersion
and never ceased to pray and hope for their return to it and for
the restoration in it of their political freedom." Both master

stories are reflected here: the phrase "never ceased to pray and hope for their return to it" mirrors the first master story, the eternal yearning of the Jewish People for their homeland; the phrase "the restoration in it [the Land of Israel] of their political freedom" draws on the second story, the concrete expression of political rights.

Later on, the Declaration goes on to express the role and values of the State. In the words, "The State of Israel will be open for Jewish immigration and for the Ingathering of the Exiles; ... it will be based on freedom, justice and peace as envisaged by the prophets of Israel," we once again hear both stories in the parallel language: "Jewish immigration" reflects the urgent and concrete modern need to absorb refugees left homeless by wars and destruction; the "Ingathering of the Exiles," while meaning the same thing, uses biblical language to refer to a process that has mystical, redemptive qualities far beyond the prosaic needs to feed and house hundreds of thousands of refugees. Similarly, the values of "freedom, justice and peace" are not just derived from the concept of modern statehood but also from the ancient story, from "the prophets of Israel." The founding fathers of the state acted in good faith in order to amalgamate the stories in their search for compromise, but many of the seeds of the political discord we live with today were sown then.

The writer Shmuel Yosef Agnon also depicted these two master stories beautifully in his short stories "The Fable of the Goat" and "From Foe to Friend," which are included in Appendix C.

## The Master Stories Collide

Both master stories of Israel are critically important today. The second story teaches the necessity of having a state, the first is the arrow pointing to where that state should be. However, neither of these stories should be, in my opinion, a guide for concrete political policy. There are those, however, who use them for this purpose.

In the early eighties I was invited to participate in a radio debate with Hanan Porat, one of the leaders of Gush Emunim, the Israeli settlement movement. The host asked us whether, as observant Jews, we referred to the State of Israel in our prayers using the phrase that describes Israel as "the beginning of the flowering of our redemption" (*reshit tzmichat ge'ulateinu*). To my surprise, we both said no, but for different reasons. I explained that I pray that "with the help of God, the State of Israel will one day *hopefully* be the flowering of our redemption," because I don't think that it has happened yet. Hanan disagreed vehemently. He believed that we were already deep inside the redemptive process. I can't be so sure. The debate between us highlighted our fundamental and differing understanding of the State of Israel and its role in history: Is it an expression of a divine, supra-historic process at work – the first master story? Or is it the result of a nationalist movement with no mythical or messianic meaning – the second?

Another difference of approach that emerged in my debate with Hanan was that he was ready to apply a master story describing the Jewish People's relationship to the Land of Israel to political questions facing the State of Israel. I believe this is a mistake. If the Jewish State is an expression of the messianic redemption, as Hanan believed, and he applied this belief to modern political issues, the question of what to do about the Palestinians is God's problem, not mine. If, however, the Jewish State is a modern nation-state that embodies the rights of a people to their own state, the Palestinian claim for national self-determination is also my problem. Similarly, for me the debate about where Israel's borders should be is only a question of relevant security and sustainability issues; for Hanan, however, the borders have been predetermined by God. He was prepared to link the master stories to political realities, while I see this as a highly problematic approach.

I believe we must live within both stories concurrently and recognize and manage the potential conflicts that arise. Both narratives add something very valuable and powerful to the whole, and there are enormous dangers of living with a single story. Unfortunately, the more extreme political parties each base their ideologies on a single story and ignore the other. I have devoted my entire career to helping Jews understand, appreciate, and live within both of these stories.

## The Three "As"

The Israeli educational system (like all educational systems) plays an important role in transferring values and culture. For many years it reflected the dominant Zionist ideology that didn't relate to the Jewish People from a positive perspective. This approach, embodied by Israelis like my kibbutznik cousin, related to Jews in the Diaspora (called the *galut* or exile) as having one of three future options: the "three As" – *aliyah* (obviously the preferred option), assimilation, or anti-Semitism. It saw nothing inherently valuable in Jewish life outside the State of Israel and expected that all Jews in the Diaspora would ultimately make *aliyah*.

As it has turned out, however, not all Jews outside Israel see these as their only options, and they have developed their own meaningful Jewish life in their Diaspora communities. My whole career has been spent dealing with the results of this reality – namely, that Jews inside and outside Israel have become distanced from each other, unable to communicate or understand each other. The "three As" were inaccurate to begin with and need to be replaced by options that are common to all members of the Jewish family. In recent years we have seen the traditional Zionist approach being replaced by a more People-focused approach based on an equal relationship between Jews wherever they are. I hope that this will strengthen the bonds between Diaspora and Israeli Jews, and I urge the State of Israel to do more to strengthen the Jewish People. There is much work to be done to bring non-Israeli Jews closer to Israel; they need to visit, to meet their extended family, to experience what it means to be part of a majority, and to appreciate how the Jewish People has adopted and adapted modern nationalism. Likewise, Israelis have a lot of work to do to appreciate being part of the Jewish People; they need to meet and talk with Jews from all over the world and to create ways in which Jews from outside Israel can be involved together with Israelis in contributing to the Jewish People and the world. I say more about this at the end of this book in relation to *Tikkun Olam*.

A strong relationship between Israelis and Diaspora Jews is central to the national security and very future of the State of Israel. Because our right to a Jewish state in Israel is justified by our being the Jewish People, when Israel or Israelis ignore the Jewish People or forget their connection, they are actually undermining our very right to have a sovereign state.

## Liking and Loving

When I was the president of Hillel and living in the US, my daughter flew to Washington, DC for a visit. At the end of our time together, I drove her to the airport. She got out of the car, gave me a big hug and a kiss, said, "Abba, I love you," and walked into the airport. Suddenly, she dropped her bags, ran back to the car, gave me another hug and kiss, and said, "Abba, I also like you." This incident made me reflect on the differences between loving and liking. It seems to me that you like someone because of the way they behave; you love someone because of the centrality of the relationship between you. I don't always like Israel; I don't always like the way the country behaves, the weather doesn't suit me, my political opinions are sometimes at odds with the government, but I never stop loving Israel, not even for a moment. If I have a strong personal relationship with the Jewish People and understand the Jewish People's relationship with Israel, then I can't help loving Israel.

## "The Nine Days of We"

I remember that during my first year living in Israel, I was walking down the street in Tel Aviv one day and suddenly the air raid sirens went off. I looked around, waiting for everyone to run, but they were all standing to attention! It was Yom HaShoah and the whole country had come to a standstill for two minutes in commemoration of an event that took place somewhere else. What was going on here?

The siren on Yom HaShoah is one example of the way in which Israel expresses its collective identity as the national home of the Jewish People. It takes place in a period of the year in which we mark the central holidays of the Jewish People in their state: the nine days linking Yom HaShoah (Holocaust Memorial Day), Yom HaZikaron (Memorial Day), and Yom HaAtzmaut (Independence Day) – a period I have termed the "Nine Days of We" to echo the traditional unit of time we call the "Days of Awe" (Rosh Hashanah and Yom Kippur). It is important to see these days as part of a unit and not just as individual days, similar to other periods of time that punctuate the Jewish calendar: the Ten Days of Repentance from Rosh Hashanah to Yom Kippur; the Three Weeks that mark the mourning period from the 17th of Tammuz to the 9th of Av; and the Omer, the redemptive period that runs from Passover to the giving of the Torah at Shavuot. There are very few celebrations or commemorations in the Jewish calendar that aren't part of a larger unit, a period of time that reflects a transition from one state to another. The "Nine Days of We" is part of this broader pattern. It is a unit of time in which we commemorate the Jewish People's collective transition, the fundamental shift from destruction and powerlessness to independence and sovereignty.

This understanding of the "Nine Days of We" explains the Yom HaShoah siren, which strangely commemorates an event that happened to one third of the Jewish People but not to Israelis and not in the geographical territory of Israel! How many other states have a national commemoration for an event that happened somewhere else? This only makes sense by viewing Israel as integrally connected to the Jewish People as a People. And it makes even more sense when we connect Yom HaShoah to the later commemorative days, which conclude with the celebration of our independence.

Unfortunately, when this approach isn't understood, both Yom HaShoah and Yom HaAtzmaut are misinterpreted: Yom HaShoah is seen as a justification for the existence of the State of Israel, and Yom HaZikaron and Yom HaAtzmaut are seen as belonging only to Israelis. This is not the way I see it. The Holocaust doesn't justify the need for a Jewish State. If you have a Jewish State, however, then obviously Yom HaShoah is important; because it is about something that happened to the Jewish People, and as the nation-state of the Jewish People we have the privilege of commemorating this experience as a majority with all the trappings of government and national expression. Yom HaShoah thus teaches me the very opposite of what my cousin Amira told me that day on Kibbutz Lahav. Rather than giving up being Jewish and becoming Israeli, if I am Israeli, I must also engage with being Jewish. Likewise, if I am Jewish and living outside Israel, I must engage with Yom HaAtzmaut to celebrate my collective connection to the national home of my People.

## Minority – Majority

During our many generations of exile, it was obvious to the Jewish People that we were a minority, living (sometimes successfully and sometimes less so) among other peoples. Being a minority deeply influenced our collective psyche. We had to nurture our distinctiveness, create our own communal institutions, and maintain connections with our People scattered across the globe. With the establishment of the State of Israel we were challenged once again to be a majority. Now we have not only influence but power; power to own the public space, to define the rules governing the lives of all citizens, and to legislate according to our values. This is a profound challenge for the Jewish People, redefining who we are and impacting all Jews, whether or not they live in the State of Israel. Having a state in which we are sovereign provides a place where Jews, both citizens and non-citizens, can experience what it means to be a majority. For Diaspora Jews this is a vital piece of their Jewish experience. When they come to Israel and immediately feel at home, they are experiencing the power of being a Jewish majority, and Israel is of enormous value because it provides this opportunity. Similarly, when Israelis travel overseas and find themselves, sometimes unintentionally, visiting Jewish communities or celebrating Jewish holidays, they realize for the first time what it means to be a minority. Both of these experiences are critical for building connections to Israel and the Jewish People as a whole.

The truth is that Israelis today are part of a collective that is both a majority and a minority. In their own state they are a majority, but they are a minority in the Muslim Middle East, and as part of the Jewish People, they are a minority in the Christian west. They live with both of these possibilities at the same time. Getting used to being a majority takes time, and they sometimes, both individually and collectively, still behave as one when they should be behaving as the other. The contemporary Israeli psychosis is not knowing what we are and making mistakes by behaving as one when we should be behaving as the other.

## Routine versus Spontaneity

Jewish tradition values both the routine and the spontaneous in Jewish life. In ways that sometimes appear to be contradictory, the rabbis used the term *keva*, which translates as "routine" or "regularity," as both positive and negative. In the Ethics of the Fathers (2:13) they teach: "When you pray, don't make your prayers fixed"; in other words, don't let your relationship with God become rote and mundane. Yet, close by in the same section (1:15), they also teach us: "Make your study of Torah regular."

These two conceptions of *keva* can be seen in the different approaches to Jewish life today in Israel and in the Diaspora. Jewish life in the Diaspora is essentially spontaneous; it isn't regulated and depends almost entirely on the free choice of the people involved. When I lived in the Diaspora, I experienced the power of three core values that are responsible for an amazingly strong Jewish life over the centuries: volunteerism, philanthropy, and community. As a result of these values, Diaspora Jews are remarkably generous and have built strong community institutions. There is great creativity and individual choice in this Jewish life; indeed, every Jew outside Israel is, perforce, a Jew by choice.

In Israel, however, Jewish life is all *keva* or regulated. Rather than volunteering out of choice, the State requires national or military service; rather than encouraging people to donate money to causes they care about, the State taxes its citizens and uses that money to fund institutions that Jews in the Diaspora fund themselves (schools, synagogues, retirement homes, etc.). And finally, the State takes responsibility for many functions traditionally run by community institutions. The government of Israel legislates a great deal about what it means to be Jewish; it defines the calendar of holidays, decides who is recognized as a rabbi, and regulates what religious services are offered and how. While there is much to be gained from this – the government pays for religious services, (some) religious rights are enshrined in the law, and Jewish culture rules the public space – we have, at the same time, lost the advantages of spontaneity according to which individuals are empowered to create their own Jewish life and to define who or what is a Jew.

As my friend Gidi Grinstein often says, Jewish life over the years depended for its survival on a network of strong Jewish communities. The State of Israel, while vitally important and essential, endangered this unique element of the Jewish People. Ironically, Ben-Gurion's concept of statehood (*mamlachtiyut*) destroyed communities. By legislating all these services, the Jewish State has actually taken over and in many ways destroyed the core methods used by Jews in other countries to create strong communities. This is an unfortunate result of the Zionist project; it has broken the voluntary nature of Jewish community and has legislated these values out of existence.

When Jews from Israel go to live in America, they don't understand the local Jewish community, precisely because they don't understand the concepts of community, philanthropy, or volunteerism. It is as if Diaspora and Israeli Jews are speaking different languages; one speaks the language of spontaneity, the other of regulation. I believe that Israel needs more spontaneity, more options, and more freedom for Jewish expressions to multiply and flourish, while Diaspora Jews would benefit from appreciating the value of *keva*. Jews in Israel have a lot to learn from their Diaspora relatives about multiple identities, about freedom, and about the value of voluntary commitment to community.

From the contradictions, similarities, and differences

between Israel and the other countries I have lived in, I extrapolate a very important principle: Jews have always made *tsimmes*. We made this "stew" – our civilization – out of the ingredients that were at hand in the cultures that surrounded us. We started with core principles and collective memories from the Torah and our history, but we always used some local seasonings to flavor our *tsimmes*. So, for example, we adopted modern nationalism and established a Jewish State, incorporating democracy and universal human rights into our existence as a People. According to my father in a book he wrote in 1940, Jews did this time after time throughout history, always borrowing ideas and principles from the mature societies and civilizations in which they lived; this, he claimed, is one of the secrets of our longevity.

Today, in Israel, I fear we have lost that ability to borrow successfully from other cultures. Either we exclude new and valuable principles, such as freedom of religion, tolerance, and democracy, because we are scared of them, or we accept everything without really testing to make sure it has lasting value. The result is a polarization in Israel between *haredi* (ultra-orthodox) Judaism, on the one hand, which is closing itself off from democracy and universal values, and secular society, on the other, which is adopting values without any filter. And both of these options are diluting the taste of our *tsimmes*, leaving it less palatable for future generations.

## Power and Powerlessness

Growing up in South Africa taught me a lot about power. Every day I would come home from school and Jacob, the servant who was almost my father's age, would be waiting to take my coat and help me take off my shoes. Then he would take me into the kitchen for the meal he had prepared for me. Lunch was not a formal meal; later, for dinner, we would all sit together to eat, and my mother would ring the bell for him to come and serve. At night he would polish my shoes and iron my school uniform. And he called me "*baas*" (boss)! That is what life was like for white South Africans at that time, and as a child I thought this was normal.

I noticed things changing when my sister started to become politically active. In the mid-1950s the prices were raised on public transportation for blacks. It was the beginning of black political organizing, which was to become outright resistance against the apartheid regime. The blacks in the townships of Johannesburg refused to take the buses and had to walk miles and miles to work. My sister was about 20 and had just got her driving license. She organized her white student friends to drive black people from their townships to work, so that they wouldn't have to take the public buses. I started to ask questions about the way things were. I once asked Jacob, "When the blacks rise up, are you going to kill us?" "No, I won't kill you," he answered, "but I will kill the white people next door. And their servant will come and kill you!" It became increasingly clear that we were doing something very wrong.

Nonetheless, it was a complicated situation. My father was vehemently opposed to apartheid, but when Israel voted against South Africa at the United Nations, he wasn't sure what to say. He agreed with Israel's vote on principle, but he feared a subsequent backlash against Jews in South Africa. As a leader of the Jewish community, he was always worried about what would happen to the Jewish People.

As a result of growing up among racism and oppression, I am determined that we must not do the same to another people. I do not believe that Israel is another apartheid; there are many differences, and I reject the direct comparison. But, as a South African, I know what can happen to a people that rules another people, and I don't want that to happen to us. I don't want my grandchildren to grow up expecting an Arab to treat them like Jacob treated me.

So, how should Israel deal with its minorities, particularly the Arabs who are Israeli citizens and the Palestinians living in the West Bank (who are not citizens)? How do we deal with the Palestinians' desire for sovereignty? If Israel is a Jewish State, what happens to non-Jews? These questions concern me greatly, and my approach to them stems from my perception of the Jews as a People, my upbringing in South Africa, and my understanding of the Holocaust.

The relationship between the State of Israel and its minorities is essentially a question of how the Jewish People deals with power. We can learn a dual lesson about this from the Holocaust – namely, what can happen when a people has no power and what can happen when a people has power. For the State of Israel this is critical. On the one hand, Israel exists because we remember being powerless and are determined that we will never suffer from powerlessness again. At the same time, however, because Israel exists, we are now in a position of power over others. As a sovereign nation with an army and the power to determine our own destiny, we must be particularly careful not to abuse that power. This is the first time in about two thousand years that we have enough power to worry about its misuse. The balance between power and powerlessness is one that we must be conscious of at all times.

I have dedicated my career to helping Jews, both Israelis and Diaspora Jews, confront the challenges of understanding Israel. We must resist the temptation to embrace only one master story or simplistic positions. Rather, we must live in the tensions of balancing the prevailing conflicts and contradictions. There is no other way for the State of Israel to sustain itself, and no other way for the Jewish People to continue to build its national home.

# 9

# America and Israel: Commonalities and Distinctions

*From my first arrival in America in 1967
as the first community shaliach of the Jewish
Agency in Baltimore, Maryland and through
the following decades, especially as the president
of Hillel, I have had the opportunity to live,
travel widely, and really get to know America.
This has been hugely powerful for me, and
I have a lifelong love of America and a deep
appreciation of the differences and similarities
between Israel and America and between
American and non-American Jews.*

*On reflecting on my relationship with
America and American Jews, it turns out that
being South African actually helped me to
understand and appreciate America.*

*I remember that in the early years of
Melitz, I looked around at the other Zionist
organizations in Israel doing Jewish identity
work with young Diaspora Jews and noticed
that they were all run by ex-South Africans.
We program directors could have met and had
a meeting in Afrikaans! Not only were we all*

*South Africans, we had all been influenced by
the same madrich (counselor) in Habonim,
Gidi Shimoni.*

*This isn't just a cute observation, it actually
tells me something about how Jews from
different places talk or don't talk to each other.
Americans have difficulty understanding
the language of Israelis; Israelis don't really
understand the language of Americans. But
we South Africans, like others who grow up in
places that imbibe the sense of tribe together
with a connection to tradition, we speak both!
And thanks to our unique perspective we can be
a bridge between American Jewish identity and
Israeli Jewish identity.*

## *Galut* – Exile

My meeting with America, after my South African and then
Israeli experiences, changed my life. As a South African Jew,
my first life experience was of being different from everybody
else. In Israel I exchanged that for a feeling of being at home,
among my own people. Then I came to America, to work with
my people in exile; but they all felt so much at home there!
So, even though the concept of *Galut* – of being in exile – had
always been an essential part of my being Jewish in the Diaspora, it was foreign to my experience in America. I realized that
American Jews, for the most part, felt that they were already
at home, whereas I grew up in South Africa feeling very different. On my frequent visits to Europe, I identified with the
Jews there who also knew that they were not really at home.

America was such a different experience that, unlike my fellow *shlichim* who were shocked by the high rate of intermarriage (somewhere around 35% at the time), I was shocked by the low rate of intermarriage.

This created two emotions in me. On the one hand, I loved America for the way it welcomed its Jews. But, at the same time, I feared America for the way it welcomed its Jews. My being in America was a constant struggle between these two emotions. Do I want American Jews to experience an-ti-Semitism in order to feel Jewish? Of course not! I want them to feel at home, but I also want them to take advantage of the right America grants them to be different. It has become clear to me that somehow the very right that America gives them to be different has the potential to nullify their very desire to be different.

In America you can be Jewish and American at the same time and the two are not contradictory – at least not for Amer-ican Jews. As a non-American Jew, though, it forced me, for the first time, to notice the distinction I felt between me as a human being and me as a Jew. As a human being, I felt very much at home in America. Yet, at the same time, I didn't feel at home there as a Jew. The two parts of my identity – the Jewish and the human – couldn't live together there; it was *galut* for me. Whereas in Israel the two parts of my identity were fully integrated and almost unnoticeable to me, in America I expe-rienced them as two very different and separate parts. I love and respect that difference which most American Jews actually don't see. They don't experience the dichotomy between being Jewish and being American, and this explains why in America, to my great surprise and contrary to my experience in South Africa and Israel, Jews really understand themselves as a reli-gion! This makes sense for American Jews of course, because if Judaism is a religion, like Christianity, then there is no national identity to express and no contradiction between being American and being Jewish.

My love and fear of America are emotions that I have carried with me ever since and that have had an enormous effect on all my subsequent work.

## Lessons from America

During my time in America I discovered the unique impact of Thomas Jefferson, and I spent much time learning about him. The idea of Jefferson and the founding fathers was brilliant: a melting pot that welcomes everyone and allows them to identify as members of their own religion but as part of the larger American people. Their bold vision particularly amazes me because they succeeded in controlling God! I have never seen any other person or country do this so well. I was already an observant Jew when I went to America, and so, for me, God was everywhere in my life; He couldn't be controlled or limited to one particular sphere. Only in America do they have the chutzpah to control God, telling Him where He is or isn't allowed. Communist regimes didn't succeed in doing this; they just got rid of Him entirely! Other countries haven't succeeded; they just let God control everything unrestrictedly. Yet, here comes America, a country that controls God, and as a result, God is a very welcome friend there; "In God we trust" they proclaim, just as long as it doesn't prevent us from limiting His influence!

This contrasts with the Jewish perspective that understands that God has limited Himself in order to empower human beings to run the world. We call this *tzimtzum*. For Jefferson and the founding fathers, it wasn't God who limited Himself, it was human beings who had the right to limit God's actions, and thus America managed to keep God out of schools and out of politics.

I find it fascinating to note that the Emancipation, during which Jews in Europe started to define themselves as a religion, coincided roughly with the establishment of the United States, which defined itself in revolutionary terms as a state in which religion was not under state control. America was therefore perfect for people who had redefined themselves as a religious group and were looking for a safe and welcoming place where all religions would be free. This has allowed Jews to be absorbed in the United States in a way unprecedented in Jewish history.

## The Idea behind the People

I was invited to teach at a famous historically black college in Atlanta. On meeting one of their history professors, I asked him from which date they start teaching American history. I wasn't sure how one defined America's starting date. Was it with Columbus in 1492 or with the Declaration of Independence in 1776? What he told me completely amazed me. "We start teaching American history," he said, "in ancient Athens with the story of an idea – democracy." America is a country whose history is actually the history of an idea. It is the same as Jewish history, which is also built on an idea, albeit a different one. As I mentioned earlier in Chapter 3, the idea that animates and drives the history of the Jewish People and their national home is God's promise to Abraham at the start of his long journey that his people, the Jewish People, will be the vehicle through which blessing will come into the world making the world a better place.

## People and State

In the world of modern nationalisms, there are two exceptions: America and Israel. Most nation-states were created by people who were living together in the same land, usually speaking the same language and sharing a culture, and who decided to build a state around themselves. In the case of America, however, it was the state that created the People. The state came first and then the People were created from the melting pot of immigrants who came from many different places. Israel, on the other hand, is an example of a People who created a state. The People came first, and despite being scattered all over the world, they managed to create a state for themselves. This ties America and Israel together; we are both profound exceptions to the rules of modern nationalism.

## Freedom

I learned about freedom in America, in two ways. First, when I understood that America was established on the principle of freedom *of* religion, I realized that, in contrast, the State of Israel was established on the principle of freedom *from* religion and that in many ways secular Zionism made freedom from religion a central part of its philosophy. Ironically it was trying to provide an ability to be Jewish without religion.

Second, in America there is real appreciation for the freedom people have to do "their own thing," as long as they are not causing harm to anyone else. You can wear a silly hat and skateboard the wrong way down Fifth Avenue and that is okay – you are just doing your own thing. Self-empowerment is a value that is deeply embedded in public life, and it is true for religion too. You can make up your own religion and practice it; you can develop your own religious expression – it is a wonderful thing. You can take the liberty provided by the Constitution and apply it to a realm in which you have decided that God rules, which we call religion; and even in that religion you still have the basic right to do your own thing.

American Judaism reflects this belief in individual autonomy and the right to create something that is personally meaningful. The danger, of course, of doing your own thing is that it begins and ends with "me," and this undermines the basic Jewish idea of memory which is fundamentally about "we." The State of Israel is the collective expression of Jewish nationalism and thus the complete antithesis of the American principles of individual freedom. Nevertheless, the more I have come to know America, the more I appreciate that both America and Israel are nation-states that do not conform to the patterns of other states, and that the Jewish People and the American People are similar to each other and also different from each other in unique and complementary ways.

# Part 2
## Peoplehood in Practice

# 10

---

## Teachers and Mentors

While Part I of this book outlines my approach to Jewish Peoplehood, Part II is about putting those ideas into practice. It is about the mentors who most impacted me, the educational approach to Peoplehood that has emerged from my experience, and the varied organizations and initiatives with which I have been involved. This section starts with a chapter about the mentors and teachers who I have been lucky enough to learn from and whose diverse approaches to Jewish Peoplehood have left a deep imprint on me. Even though this chapter could have been placed earlier in the book, reflecting their different approaches to Jewish Peoplehood, I have decided to place the chapter here, as the opening section of Part II, in order to emphasize that each one of these memorable people was first and foremost an educator. Indeed, many of them wouldn't have known (or even agreed with) the term "Jewish Peoplehood," but I have no doubt that they took their own passion for the Jewish People, concretized it, and passed it on to me. Together, their accumulated wisdom provoked, supported, and enriched my thinking, so that I could put my own passion into practice, as described in the chapters that follow.

It is truly a blessing to have people to learn from, and I have been blessed many times throughout my career. For years I have told stories about some of these mentors, while others have remained silently in the background, influencing my work and thinking but not visible to others. In this essay I want to honor them all by acknowledging their contribution and drawing out universal lessons about the power of teachers and mentors for all of us.

## My Father: Zvi Infeld

I remember clearly the last conversation that I had with my father. It was a Shabbat morning in December 1978, and I knew that he was not long for this world. It was just the two of us in his room at Tel HaShomer hospital, and I asked him the question – part of our ongoing, life-long conversation – "Abba, is there a minimum that a Jew has to know in order to be a Jew?"

For me, my father was, and in many ways still is, the real, authentic, quintessential Jew. He embodied what I think of as "Jewish," and he expressed it right in front of me. He was the authoritative source about Judaism and Jewish life of my childhood, and his approach to Jewishness made an impression that remains with me today, even after I have chosen my own path which diverges in some ways from his. To me, my father was a Jew in every cell of his being; his identity was entirely Jewish and not the multiple or shifting identities that we talk about today. Born in 1899, he was of a different century; a Jew and nothing else, completely committed, intellectually consistent, and highly idiosyncratic.

I thought that his answer to my question there in his hospital room would be related to the Hebrew language, a Zionist idea, or a rabbinic text – all subjects that he was passionate about. But instead, he answered in a very broad and enigmatic way: "Of course there is a minimum. A Jew has to know more today than he knew yesterday."

Zvi Infeld was born in a small town called Novysanz in Galicia. He was one of nine children in a religious Chasidic household and moved with his family to Vienna in his teens. My father left Orthodoxy in those years, under the influence of the secular and nationalist Jewish movements that were swirling through Europe in the early twentieth century. He became part of Hashomer Hatzair, the secular Zionist youth movement, where he translated the passion and fervor of Chasidim into a secular, nationalistic context. For my father being a Chasid or being a Zionist were essentially the same thing: they were both expressions of being Jewish, but he was sure that only one would ensure that the Jewish People could survive the threats of anti-Semitism and assimilation.

In 1924, in his early twenties, my father left Vienna and went to Bulgaria as a *shaliach* of Hashomer Hatzair, aiming to establish the youth movement and a Hebrew school and thus connect Bulgarian Jews to Zionism and the Jewish People. He recruited eight Hebrew-language teachers in Israel to fulfill this mission. One of them was Olga Genn, born in Poland, who had made *aliyah* to Israel as a student and who had graduated from Seminar Levinsky, the first teacher training college in Palestine. She later became my mother.

My parents were in Bulgaria until around 1929, when they moved to South Africa to open a Jewish school. Despite staying in South Africa for over 30 years, they both maintained the mentality of temporary visitors on a mission for the People at large. They worked as teachers, raised me and my sister, Tamara, and over time my father became the professional head of the Zionist movement in South Africa and a leader in the community.

In 1940 my father wrote a book called *Israel in the Decline of the West*, a critique of the book *The Decline of the West* by the historian Oswald Spengler, which argued for a cyclic approach to history in which cultures are born, mature, and decay. Like Spengler, my father believed that cultures develop in stages, and in his book he outlined the way that the Jewish People has evolved and developed over millennia. For him the stories of the patriarchs and matriarchs reflected the childhood of the Jewish People, the stories of Joshua and the Kings were adolescence, the Prophets symbolized full maturity, and with the Rabbis we reached old age. For my father, the Jewish People is an exception to Spengler's theory, as it doesn't die at this point but rather engages with other surrounding civilizations that are at earlier stages of development and incorporates from them valuable ideas, such as modern nationalism, that allowed the People to flourish and develop further. My father believed, prophetically, that the Jewish People in 1940 was on the edge of both physical and metaphorical annihilation, and he saw Zionism as a way of saving them and guaranteeing their future. I was born after the publication of this book, but these ideas were still having an enormous impact on my father throughout my childhood. Current events were a validation of ideas he had been thinking about for years, and he was watching his theory play out in front of his eyes.

As a secular Zionist in South Africa my father was quite unusual. On his 70th birthday, the chief rabbi of South Africa, Rabbi Louis Rabinowitz, made a speech to honor him: "Zvi Infeld is the most consistent individual I have ever known. Of South African Jewish leaders, a large number made *aliyah* to Israel. They all went to synagogue in South Africa, but the vast majority of them stopped going when they got to Israel. Zvi Infeld never went to synagogue in South Africa and never went in Israel!" Many years later I visited Port Elizabeth, where my parents had lived for a few years and where my father was principal of the Hebrew School. By virtue of that position a seat in the synagogue had been designated for him. The old man who looks after the synagogue today took me around and showed me the seat with the plaque inscribed with the name Zvi Infeld. It meant a great deal to me to sit in that seat, especially when the old man told me that I was the first Infeld to ever sit in it!

I sometimes wonder about my father's restrained response to the Holocaust. His mother, brother, and nephew were all killed in Auschwitz, and yet he never personalized it. For him the Holocaust was almost inevitable in the scheme of Jewish history, a theoretical part of his ideological approach to the world. His response to the Holocaust was to take action, particularly in the Zionist movement. For example, in 1948, my father was sent by Ben-Gurion to meet Jan Smuts, then prime minister of South Africa, and to persuade the South African government to sell fighter planes to the nascent Jewish State. In the midst of an election campaign, Smuts couldn't show such public support for the Jewish State, but he agreed to give the Zionist Federation "postal rights" to deliver mail to Israel and gave them fighter planes to use for the delivery, which then got "stuck" in Israel for a while!

My father's whole life was dedicated to the Jewish People, and he served them with his whole being. He was my first teacher and, even though I have lived more of my life without him than with him, he has never ceased teaching and influencing me.

## Isidore Kahanowitz

I had two history teachers in school. One was a classic old-school teacher who would walk into class, open a book, and read through it with us to prepare for the test. There was no conversation, no interaction, and no real education going on. The second was Isidore Kahanowitz, a master educator who taught me to love history.

One time he came into class and threw me a piece of chalk. "Infeld grab that, " he said. Then he asked me to draw a line around all four walls of the classroom. I felt like an idiot drawing a line which went across the board and all around the walls. When I was finished and he had everyone's attention, he highlighted a very small section of the longer line. "This," he said, pointing to the long line, "is the history of the world, and this tiny little piece," indicating his short section, "is how much we know of it. What do you imagine happened in the rest of the time? What chance is there that something you do today will impact someone in 50 more years? It is very easy to learn about events, but the important thing is to discover what happened and think about how those events are going to influence the future."

I fell in love with history at that moment. Suddenly history was relevant to me and I was relevant to it. Kahanowitz taught me that whatever I do today, my great-great-great grandchildren will learn as history. So, whether I like it or not, something is going to be passed from one generation to another, and it is up to me what that will be. That lesson, which he demonstrated to all of us though the chalk line on the wall, lies behind everything I speak about as a Jewish educator.

He had a habit in his classroom that you had to have your bag right next to your desk, and if it was left in the middle of the aisle he would walk by and kick it out of the way. So the mischievous kids, including myself, decided to test him. We took a bag and put it in the middle of the room and filled it with bricks. As he came by he kicked it out the way and consequently hurt his foot. The class broke into laughter, seeing that the joke had been successful. His first response was: "Who *didn't* laugh?" One of the nerdy kids, of course, put up his hand. Kahanowitz said, "I thought that was very funny. I don't need people who don't laugh in my class." He bought our hearts in that small moment, because he took advantage of an unexpected situation, a paradox – a teacher kicks something, he hurts his foot, and he turns it into a moment of education – laughter is good, laughter is important, help the group bond, don't be supportive of those who are trying to break the bond between people. I learned all of that from one little kick.

Even though I have already made it clear that memory is really important to me, this does not in any way reduce the power of history, which is relevant because living with the consciousness that whatever you do today will be the history of the future makes you behave very differently.

Even after more than 50 years, Isidore Kahanowitz remains for me the model of what an educator should be. He had a knack for taking seemingly simple events and creating moments of education out of them. He could teach profound life lessons by exploiting the natural curiosity of his students.

## Rabbi David Sanders

It was the late 1950s. I was a teenager on my way to the Norwood Swimming Pool on a Sunday morning and looking for a ride. A young man in his 20s, wearing a *kippah*, pulled up to give me a ride, and introduced himself as Rabbi David Sanders. I remember his American accent, and the funny way he spoke English! He wanted to know if I was Jewish and if I had heard of the Talmud and was amazed to hear that I learned Talmud every week with my father. Rabbi Sanders was in South Africa to start a yeshiva and saw me as a perfect target. He invited me for Shabbat, and I went to his yeshiva where I studied Talmud for the first time with people my own age. I found it very inspiring and even moved into the yeshiva for a few months. I became more observant of Shabbat, although often it depended on what movie was playing at the cinema on Saturday afternoon! Through my learning with Rabbi Sanders I found more and more ways to express myself as a Jew. He gave me the "rhythm" of being Jewish; the ease and confidence that allowed me to fit into a warm, religious Jewish community. Until this point my experience of Judaism had been an idiosyncratic reflection of my father's intellectual, secular Zionism; Rabbi Sanders helped to thicken that Jewish experience to include religion. With his help I became a practitioner of Judaism, an enriching perspective that remains with me until this day and allows me to handle myself everywhere and with all types of

Jews and to deeply appreciate the religious aspects of Jewish life.

## Shulamit Katznelson

It was the mid-1960s, and I was working in Tel Aviv for the Jewish Agency. One day, out of the blue, I got a call from Shulamit Katznelson. Shulamit was a member of one of Israel's elite founding families and firmly on the right of the political spectrum. Due to her political views she strongly believed that we had to find ways to live with the Arabs in our midst, and she founded Ulpan Akiva, a unique institution in Netanya, for teaching Hebrew to adults, both Jews and non-Jews. She said she wanted to meet me. "I am going to be in Tel Aviv tomorrow morning. Can you meet me there and drive me to Netanya?" So I met her on Rehov Allenby, where she went shopping for a handbag and kept me waiting for an hour, and on the way to Netanya we talked about many important things. She was basically interviewing me for a job at Ulpan Akiva.

The first lesson I learned from Shulamit, in my new position as coordinator of extracurricular activities, was that teaching is the imparting of knowledge; education is something else. She believed that work with adults is not about educating them but about creating contexts in which they can educate themselves. The official reason for the existence of Ulpan Akiva, and the basis for its government funding, was to teach Hebrew. However, its real purpose was to create contexts for important things to happen between diverse people. For example, even though ostensibly serving new immigrants, Ulpan Akiva also taught Hebrew to Jewish tourists visiting Israel. It also taught Hebrew to Israeli Arabs and Arabic to Israeli Jews. Shulamit showed me that real education comes from meeting and living with people different from ourselves, and she managed to take advantage of the uniqueness of Israel by bringing three populations together: Israeli Jews, Israeli (and non-Israeli) Arabs, and Jewish tourists. Immediately after the Six Day War, for example, Shulamit arranged for 50 Arab doctors from Gaza to come and learn Hebrew. I found myself teaching them Agnon and other Hebrew literature! She gave me a deep respect for the Arab world and an understanding that we have to live here together.

Shulamit saw encounters between different people as a way of creating a different world. She helped me understand that we are only fully ourselves when we are contrasted with the other and that the meeting between ourselves and the other can lead to amazing experiences and contexts for education. Working for her was a very important part of my life.

## Morele (Mordechai) Bar'On

While I was working at Ulpan Akiva by day and going to law school in Tel Aviv at night, I was offered the chance to go to America as a community *shaliach* in Baltimore, Maryland. I arrived there as Morele Bar'On was appointed the head of the Youth and Hechalutz Department of the Jewish Agency, and he became my direct boss. I had known Morele in the army when he was the head of the IDF Education Unit and I was a lowly soldier doing my military service. I was already in awe of him.

Morele was very creative. Until he came along, all the Jewish Agency *shlichim* were working in the Zionist youth movements. He looked at that structure and, from a rare concern (at the time) with the rest of the Jewish world, he added *shlichim* in Jewish community centers and other places where Jews were, not just traditional Zionist institutions. His creativity inspired me to do all kinds of crazy things that would serve the whole Jewish People. For example, I was in Baltimore one day and drove past Mount St. Agnes College, a convent.

I was curious about it, so I went in and offered to teach Israeli dancing to the nuns. They thought I was out of my mind! But I wanted to bring Israel to as many different populations as possible. I formed the Mount St. Agnes Israeli Folk Dance Troupe, and I went every week and taught them the dances. They became famous throughout Baltimore and gave many performances, attracting also Jews and increasing their connection to Israel. Morele sent me a note about this, proud of me for thinking out of the box and not sticking to rigid patterns.

Another example of how he inspired me was one of the first activities I did with the *madrichim* of the youth movements. It was a few months after the Six Day War, after which Yitzhak Rabin had made a powerful victory speech. I took his speech, which Morele had actually written, and juxtaposed it with the ancient speech of Elazar Ben Yair, the leader of the Jews at Masada two thousand years earlier. I told the *madrichim* that both of these were the speeches of Elazar, written for two eventualities: the first in the case of surrender, the second in the case of victory. It was an amazing activity, and inspired by Morele's words.

Morele knew how to listen and always had new and resourceful answers to problems. He would really pay attention, ask questions, and engage in real discussion. He also influenced my political thinking more than anyone else. He embodied a combination of modern liberal values and Jewish nationalism; he was liberal and open-minded with deep sense of pride and great love for the Jewish People. He was not a religious Jew in the traditional sense, but as a result of the Six Day War in which he had served as a senior officer, he had embarked on his own Jewish journey, developing his relationship with Jewish texts and customs. He had his own ideas about how a people could develop their own *mitzvot*, even without a God commanding them from the outside.

Morele exemplified for me what it is to be a "real Israeli" in a way that I could never be. After all, I was just a kid from South Africa, a lowly soldier, with no military distinctions at all and here was Morele, a secular Zionist, born and bred in the Land, Moshe Dayan's right-hand man, a senior officer during the Six Day War. Despite this background he was also, rather unusually, dedicated to the Jewish People, working in the Jewish Agency and developing new kinds of *shlichut*, working with the non-Zionist world of American Jewry. Morele gave me access to a level of the Israeli establishment that I would otherwise never have had, and he introduced me to amazing people, such as Moshe Sharett, Golda Meir, and others. One of them was Shlomo Bardin, who also became a great influence on me.

## Shlomo Bardin

It was spring of 1970, I was finishing my *shlichut* in Baltimore and Morele sent me to the Brandeis Bardin Institute in southern California for a month. The Brandeis Bardin Institute had been established by an Israeli educator called Shlomo Bardin who, with the help of Judge Louis Brandeis, had bought a large piece of land in Simi Valley, California – the largest piece of land owned by a Jewish institution outside the State of Israel – and founded a program, which is still running, to give young Jews with very little Jewish knowledge or connection an intense, immersive Jewish experience for four weeks every summer.

Shlomo told me that he wanted me to do two things: teach about Israel for half an hour a day and spend the rest of the time talking to the students. Most importantly he told me to "talk to them but never ask them 'what is this place doing to you?' Just let things happen." He made me promise that I would listen more than I would talk. Just like Shulamit Katznelson, Shlomo believed in creating contexts for important things to happen.

And indeed, I spent most of my time there talking and listening, just having informal conversations. This taught me something very important – namely, we build relationships by talking about ourselves to others. From Shlomo I learnt the importance of personal stories in Jewish education. "What is intimacy?" he asked me. "It is the ability to reveal yourself in front of someone else, to build a relationship." I thus learned to tell stories about myself in order to stimulate the relationship, and then, as soon as the other person started talking, to start listening. Shlomo kept reminding me to listen more than talk. Melitz was born out of this profound lesson and his deep influence.

## Rabbi David Hartman

Rabbi David Hartman, in my eyes one of the past generation's greatest Jewish philosophers, was a unique rabbi and educator. When you walked into his study, it was immediately clear that he embodied the integration of Jewish and general philosophy. He had so many books with different colored covers, the black and gold-covered Jewish books on one side and the more colorful philosophy books on the other, and he had mastery of both. He could pick up Kant or the Talmud and talk about both and how they complemented each other.

I learned from him that the art of the Jewish People is the art of commentary. If the Germans have literature and art, the Jews have interpretation. We have, unfortunately, stopped living our art form. David Hartman was a revival of the form. He could take a text and read it with a contemporary sensibility, giving it meaning for today just as Rashi did with his commentary in the eleventh century. It was both timeless and a product of its time. He wasn't bound by other commentators or what had come before. He had to know them, and he did, but he wasn't constricted by them. He never gave up his right to be a commentator like them, and he demanded others do the same. He taught me to love the text, not because of what it says but because of what it could say if read correctly. That was his greatness.

David appreciated wisdom from outside Jewish life and used it in order to read Jewish texts and make them meaningful: "I don't understand the dichotomy between being Jewish and being democratic," he would say, "for me it is both and that is who I am." So when he read a Jewish text he brought to it all of his sensibilities. The same text could be read by someone else who didn't share his democratic values and the interpretation would be totally different. David read everything with his whole self.

My first Rebbe, David Sanders, introduced me to the commentaries of the past; they were there to be learned and respected and couldn't be touched. My father, on the other hand, always told me that it was our job to write the next commentaries, the next chapters of the Jewish People's story. For me, David Hartman was the religious Jew and Morele Bar'On was the secular Jew trying to do just that. Both of them touched responsive chords in me and inspired me with their efforts and for that I felt great love for the two of them.

## Michael Rosenak

Mike Rosenak was the educational adviser to the Youth and Hechalutz Department when I worked for the Jewish Agency. During the early years of Melitz we ran summer camps for Israeli and American kids in the north of Israel and Mike came with his family to staff these camps. He exemplified for the kids and the staff so many qualities: humility, knowledge, commitment to education, and an openness to listen and learn. Mike lived with an a priori commitment to Jewish law. He was bound by it in all that he did and that freed his mind. He said:

"If you really want people to think freely, you have to let them know that there is a distinction between what goes on in their head and what they actually do." He was intellectually honest, and his mind had no limitations.

I have never seen such honesty and humility in a person. More than anything else, I learned from Mike that education is not a job but a mission, a calling or *shlichut*. Mike taught education as if it were an academic discipline, but really he was teaching you how to carry out a *mitzvah*. When I listened to him talking about education, I was reminded of Rabbi Sanders teaching me how to make a blessing on a *lulav*. They were both teaching me how to carry out a *mitzvah*, each in their unique and individual way.

I find it very hard to read Mike's books; his language is beautiful yet difficult, and sometimes hard to understand. But I return to them again and again, because even though I may not understand the whole paragraph, I always find a sentence that makes sense to me and then I know that he is talking to me.

## My Mother: Olga Infeld

I end this chapter by talking about the person who probably had the greatest influence on me of all: my mother. Olga Infeld was recruited by my father to be a Hebrew teacher in Bulgaria and went with him to Africa, where they were married. She spent most of her life as a teacher, and while for some years she also ran a dress shop to supplement their meager teacher salaries, her greatest influence was as a Jewish educator. She was the first head of Jewish Studies at the first Jewish day school in South Africa, quite a radical appointment as she wasn't a traditionally observant Jew. She taught generations of students, and even after retiring in her 80s, she continued teaching Hebrew to Russian immigrants in Israel as a volunteer.

She initiated the idea of bat mitzvah ceremonies for girls in South Africa. Bat mitzvah ceremonies were unheard of at the time, and because the rabbinical authorities wouldn't allow them to take place inside the synagogue, she took them outside. She connected the bat mitzvah to the holiday of Shavuot, because of the story of the Book of Ruth which we read on that holiday, and every year on Shavuot, all the girls who had turned 12 years old that year celebrated their bat mitzvah. It was, at first, a challenge to the establishment but was eventually adopted widely across the country.

Most important of all, however, my mother taught me about love. She was a never-ending well of bubbling love, optimism, and positive thinking. While other people taught me about honesty, about Judaism, and about education, she taught me about love. It was the love that she gave me that pushed me toward all my other mentors and enabled me to combine their lessons into a single approach.

All my work reflects the philosophies of these teachers and mentors. They were all different and didn't all get along with each other, but I took something from each of them. They emerged at critical points in my life, as a young adult and, particularly, during the formative years of Melitz, and had enormous influence on everything I have done since in every institution and with every educational program I have been involved with.

# 11

## Educational Moments and Jewish Education

*My father came to visit me in Baltimore in 1968, and we went for a walk in a Jewish neighborhood. We sat down on a bench which was advertising Levinson's Funeral Home. My father didn't know what a funeral home was; in South Africa, we had the hevra kadisha, a traditional burial society. I explained that a funeral home is a private business which takes care of you after death. "I don't know exactly what you are doing here in America," he said, "but you will know if you are successful when they change the name from 'Funeral Home' to 'Institutes of Graduation from Jewish Education,' because the only way you can graduate from Jewish education is by dropping dead." This lesson has stayed with me all these years. Jewish education is a central part of Jewish life and there is no such as thing as "graduation." You are never finished, until the last moment of your life.*

## Educating toward Peoplehood

Perhaps because both of my parents were teachers, it has always seemed to me that education is an important way to work for and with the Jewish People. And, despite a short foray into law school, and my father's long-forgotten dreams that I become a physicist, education has been the focus of my career. Jewish education, though, often implies images of traditional-looking teachers in Jewish day schools or synagogues teaching history or holidays. This is the absolute antithesis of the approach to education which I have practiced and developed throughout my career and which was ultimately designed – no matter the setting or institution – to foster a sense of belonging to the Jewish People with all the components described in Part I.

## *Limmud* (Learning) versus *Chinuch* (Education)

My fundamental approach to education stems from insights embedded in the Hebrew language. In Hebrew, the word for education is *chinuch*. It is related to the words Chanukah or *chanukat habayit* (house-warming), which refer to the notion of dedication. Thus, the moment of education is the moment in which you dedicate your mind to something and, as a result, your behavior shifts. I understand this to be fundamentally different from learning and teaching, which comes from the Hebrew word *limmud*. The roots of the words *lilmod* (to learn) and *lelamed* (to teach) are related, and both refer to the transmission of information and skills – namely, the process of acquiring knowledge. The reflexive form of the root of *limmud* is rarely used. Rather, *limmud* is essentially about someone giving you something; it is directional and external to yourself. *Chinuch*, on the other hand, often appears in the reflexive form *lehitchanech* meaning to become educated, which is a reflexive process. And something that is reflexive also becomes reflective. It is about internal change. If the purpose of *limmud* is to ensure what you know, the purpose of *chinuch* is to choose what you should dedicate your life and actions to. *Limmud* is the imparting of information and skills for life; *chinuch* is providing meaning for life. We all need knowledge; we can't live without it. But what really motivates how we live and the choices we make are the moments of education we experience and not the knowledge we have acquired.

I understand teaching and education as interrelated but separate concepts that each require their own method. The best way to transmit information and skills is through a structured process of learning: linear, organized, and developmentally appropriate. A person acquires one piece of knowledge and builds on it with additional facts, adding more and more information as time goes on in a logical order that leads to mastery of a body of knowledge. I learn about differential equations after I learn basic numerical concepts, so that the learning process is logical and successful. Education, on the other hand, is not about acquiring information or facts. It is about developing memories, cultivating feelings, attaching those feelings to concepts, and, ultimately, cultivating behaviors that derive from beliefs. If we "do" education in the way we "do" learning – standardized, logical, and linear – it won't work, because people are all different, experience emotional processes individually, and experience things (even the same course of events) differently. I have thus come to believe that education is achieved through experiences and educational moments.

### Educational Moments

One of my most powerful educational moments was when I was about 16 years old. It was just before Yom Kippur, and I was rushing to get ready to go to synagogue. My father was in the living room reading the newspaper. He called me in. "You are not going to *shul* until you bring me your last report card."

We both knew that my latest report card testified to the fact that I wasn't a very good student. I brought the report card, and my father took out his lighter and burnt it to ash. Then he said: "You want to know what Yom Kippur is all about? It is what I have just done. Your past does not have to ensure your future. You can do things differently, and if you understand that, you have understood Yom Kippur." That was a moment of education.

At Melitz we held summer camps for Israeli and American teenagers. On one occasion there were 150 Israelis at a camp, ready to meet their American peers. The Israelis were all English-speaking, largely secular, middle-class kids; the Americans were all from NFTY, the Reform movement youth organization. The Americans were delayed, and everyone was waiting for them, eager to start the activities. When they finally arrived, we went to have lunch. There were 300 Jewish kids in the dining room, and I couldn't tell who were Israelis and who were Americans. To me, they all looked the same in their similar style jeans and sneakers, until the end of the meal, when the American reform rabbi stood up, banged on the table, and called for "the *birkat*" as *birkat hamazon* (Grace After Meals) is commonly known in some American summer camps. Every one of the Americans started singing in Hebrew in harmony. The other 150 people in the room had no idea what was going on; they had never heard it, they didn't know the tune, and yet they were the only ones in the room who actually understood the words! That was a profound educational moment, and I immediately sent the counselors to sit with their groups and ask the question, what just happened? As a result, the American teenagers asked the Israelis, what kind of Jew are you? Why don't you know *birkat hamazon*? When did you last go to synagogue? The Israeli teenagers, in return, asked the Americans, what kind of Jew are you? Do you understand the language that you just chanted? It is this kind of conversation that is at the heart of education.

In more examples than I can count and in every framework I have worked in, I have seen that education is made up of educational moments which happen throughout the course of a person's life in no particular order and without clear progression. Rather than a linear process that leads a person from lack of knowledge to acquisition of knowledge, educational moments are serendipitous and unpredictable, leading in a zigzag from one insight and understanding of the world to another.

When a person experiences something that is surprising or unknown – how can Israeli teenagers know Hebrew but have never heard of *birkat hamazon* or why is my father burning my mediocre report card? – a moment of education can take place. In that moment is a recognition that something is strange or does not align with our previous understanding or expectation, and it raises questions and confusion. The key to *chinuch* is encountering, and most importantly, paying attention to what is going on around us and noticing the paradoxes that arise. It is from these moments of education that a person develops new understandings of the world that then impact their behavior. This is the education I believe in: the process of change that comes from encountering, noticing, and incorporating new understandings of life's paradoxes.

## Educational Spaces

If educational moments are the key components of transformative education, it becomes clear why the best Jewish education takes place in camps, Israel trips, and other informal settings. When participants on an Israel trip experience Israel as both familiar and unfamiliar, they have to ask themselves who they are and what it means to be Jewish. When campers live for several weeks in a distinctive (almost magical) reality which is so different from their home environment, it is possible to prompt questions of meaning and identity and experiment with new behaviors.

This also explains why schools have limited potential to educate, in the sense of *chinuch*, although they can certainly provide *limmud*. Schools traditionally transmit knowledge that society considers important and play a very important role in socializing children. In order to accomplish that, they are fundamentally about uniformity; they provide the same information and experiences to all students, regardless of their capacities, memories, or backgrounds. And precisely because they are not able to take account of the individual experiences of each student, traditional schools struggle to do *chinuch*. We cannot rely on them to perform that function; schools should be seen as settings that strengthen, support, or complement places where education can take place most naturally – namely, the *chinuch* that happens in camps, youth groups, and families. This is the approach my father taught me; he would always prefer me to miss school rather than a youth movement meeting.

## The Role of the Educator

I met a young woman who was on an Israel trip. She came up to me after I gave a lecture to her group, heartbroken that she hadn't felt anything during her group's visit to the Kotel. While the rest of the group appeared to have had an amazing experience there, it just didn't affect her, and she felt that she was doing something wrong. "That is wonderful!" I told her. I then asked her about other positive experiences she had had during the trip, and she launched into a long list of things, including some amazing contradictions she had noticed and new insights she had arrived at.

What happened here and what role should an educator play in maximizing the educational moment? First, the counselors had clearly imposed their own interpretation on the experience and were so busy telling everyone how amazing it was going to be that they didn't let this woman have her own experience. Second, the counselors didn't seem to notice that this woman was not responding to the experience in the same way as the rest of the students. They treated all the students as if they were the same, trying to create a shared group experience, which is impossible, at the expense of the students' individual experiences. It would have been more effective and powerful if, on noticing people's different reactions to the Kotel, they had staged another experience – a conversation about the varied feelings and opinions.

The role of an educator in education is absolutely critical. It is the educator's role to create an ever-growing number of educational moments for an ever-growing number of people. Good educators do this in several ways. First and foremost, they get to know their students and love them. This is the base requirement for helping students feel part of the Jewish family. The conversations that educators have with their students are important experiences in themselves, especially when there is real dialogue and storytelling.

In addition to crafting conversations, educators play an important role in staging and facilitating experiences. They build stimulating activities, plan memorable itineraries, and facilitate productive discussions in which diverse voices are brought into the discussion. Good educators also have an enhanced capacity to notice everything around them. They pay close attention to things that the learners either take for granted or don't (yet) understand and then ask questions about those things. They ensure the noticeability of the things around them that don't fit with previous assumptions and thus help their students develop their own sensitivity to contradictions and paradoxes.

Last, good educators know that educational moments are

highly individual, and so they are sensitive to the individual pace with which students move to new understandings. Unlike the case of the student at the Kotel, they don't rush or push, and they never assume that one student's experience is the same as another's.

## The Practice of Good Education: Storytelling

There was once a dog called Judy. She was a beautiful dog with a white coat. She was my dog, and everybody loved her. One day Judy tried to get into the house, and the door was locked. She couldn't get in. So she climbed up on the roof and came down through the chimney. Because the chimney was full of soot, Judy came out of the chimney totally black. Now nobody recognized Judy, they didn't know she was the same dog, and they didn't like her. She suffered terribly. Until one day, my father was watering the garden, and Judy came running out to the grass and ran through the water. All the soot was washed away, and everyone realized that it was Judy who had been the black dog!

    This is a story that I made up for my grandchildren. It is a simple story, one of a series that I tell them about Judy, my beloved dog. This story carries important messages about judging people based on the color of their skin, and more. I could easily have told them that all human beings are the same, but the power of the story is much greater. It creates a relationship; the listeners feel that they know and have a relationship with Judy. Then they connect their emotions to the lessons, and the learning is very powerful. The stories that we tell create memories, and these connect to our emotions. They are one of the best tools in an educator's tool box. I use stories all the time.

## The Practice of Good Education:
## Content Facilitation

At Melitz we pioneered an educational practice called "content facilitation" and trained generations of educators in it. For me, this is a blueprint for an authentic Jewish discussion in which the facilitator starts by recognizing that participants are not empty vessels waiting to be "filled" by expert teachers; they are complex and unique individuals who bring their own set of memories and experiences to the conversation. Accordingly, good educators start with the participants themselves and what they know and already think, an approach that reflects basic respect for the learners. Their memories and experiences are to be welcomed into the conversation and to form part of it. It is similarly valuable for the educator to bring their own authentic self into the conversation.

And what does an authentic Jewish discussion look like? I learned from my friend and colleague Udi Leon that a Jewish discussion has three basic characteristics and they all emerge from the Talmud. They are the "Three Cs": collective, contextual, and conflictual. First, the discussion always relates to the collective. It is about or for the community and focuses on helping people connect to the "we." Second, the discussion is not theoretical but deals with what is relevant to the Jewish People living in a specific time and place. Third, the discussion always brings more than one approach for consideration, which is why the Talmud brings both the majority and the minority opinions. In other words, a true Jewish discussion takes place among a people (communal), about a people (context), and with more than one potential direction or opinion (conflict) – just like a Talmud page where there is a 900-year-old conversation going on between rabbis who are "talking" across time and space about the same subject. The goal of a true Jewish discussion is a situation where we are all challenging each other in our attempt to uncover and understand the paradoxes, disagreements, and assumptions that lie between us. This is not a monologue – if it were, we would ignore the voices of the learners. Likewise, it isn't dialogue – for that we don't need a facilitator or a variety of voices. It is rather a "groupologue."

## The Practice of Good Education: Embracing the Fog of Complexity

Almost every year when I was running Melitz we were invited to appear at the Knesset Education Committee and report on the work we were doing, which was heavily funded by the Ministry of Education. I found that all the committee members were happy to tell me that each of their kids, be they from right- or left-wing families, had had a great experience in our seminars. Each one had found a teacher with whom they could identify, as every point of view was always represented. I was happy that, even though the kids had found people like themselves to identify with, they were also exposed to opposing opinions and multiple perspectives, which was our main intention. We were not afraid of debate; we didn't want to lift the fog of complexity and leave everyone with a clear picture, because there are no simple answers. The world we live in is complex and unclear; we can't ignore that fact but can only teach from within it. We learn this from the Torah which tells us: "And Moses approached the thick cloud (in Hebrew, *arafel*) because that is where God is" (Exodus 20:18). It is telling us not to fear the complexity of what we cannot fully understand but rather to get closer to it, for that is where the truth lies. The teacher who always wants to define and simplify and explain away the difficulties is doing a disservice to the student and to the realities of life. Yet, the educator who embraces complexity and facilitates the creation of educational moments is truly doing critical work that contributes to the continued significant renaissance of the Jewish People.

# 12

## Hillel and Shammai: Models of Peoplehood Educators

As I have argued in various places throughout this book, I believe that the educational process is at its most effective when a good educator is really paying attention to the questions asked by their students and listens to what is behind their words. I have not only seen this in practice countless times throughout my career, but I have also learned similar lessons from three powerful stories that appear next to each other in Tractate Shabbat 31a in the Talmud (see Appendix B for the full text). Each story is about a potential convert who goes to the famous rabbis Hillel and Shammai and has very different experiences with each.

In the first story, a non-Jew (in Hebrew, *nochri*) goes to Shammai and asks to become Jewish. He asks Shammai, "How many Torahs do you have?" Shammai answers truthfully, "We have two: the written Torah and the oral Torah." The nochri demands of Shammai, "Accept me as a Jew and teach me only the written Torah." Shammai rejects him outright. The *nochri* then goes to Hillel and makes the same demand. Hillel immediately accepts him.

In the second story, a potential proselyte comes to Shammai and demands, "Teach me the whole Torah while I stand on one foot." Again, Shammai's response is rejection. The *nochri* goes to Hillel, and Hillel says to him the famous statement: "What is hateful to you, you shouldn't do to others. All the rest is commentary. Now go and learn." In most versions of the story, it is not stated explicitly that Hillel accepts him.

The third story describes that a non-Jew is walking outside the study hall and hears a discussion about some of the laws of the Temple, particularly the beautiful clothes of the High Priest. He decides he wants to become the High Priest, presumably so that he will get the clothes. He goes to Shammai and asks to be accepted on condition that he be appointed High Priest. Based on his commitment to truth (that it is indeed impossible for a proselyte to become a High Priest), Shammai (again) rejects him outright and rebuffs him with a builder's cubit (probably some kind of ruler used in construction). Hillel accepts him immediately and then tells him to go and learn. Specifically, Hillel tells him to go and learn the laws of the Temple, where he discovers the law that anyone except the High Priest who comes close to the Holy of Holies will be struck down. The *nochri* asks who this law applies to, and on being told that it applied to King David, he reasons that if such a great king was liable to this kind of punishment and couldn't become the High Priest, all the more so will he not be able to achieve this status.

These stories raise a number of educational questions. First, why does the Talmud bring three different stories? Wouldn't one suffice? Regarding the behavior of Hillel and Shammai in each of the stories, is there a difference between their responses to the different potential Jews, what is behind their responses, and what are we supposed to learn from them? If the purpose was simply to show that Shammai was more strict than Hillel, one would have sufficed. I believe that through the differences between Hillel and Shammai we learn something fundamental about good education. In the first story, Hillel and Shammai hear the *nochri's* request very differently and behave accordingly. Shammai hears the request and rejects him on the basis that he doesn't have the right to set his own conditions. Hillel, however, does something very differ-ent. He first of all asks himself about the potential Jew stand-ing in front of him, namely, who is he and what is he looking for? Hillel takes the *nochri's* response to mean that he is happy to take on the authority of God but cannot accept the authority of the rabbis. Hillel's response to this reflects a core principle of the twentieth-century philosopher John Dewey: know when to trust yourself as a teacher. Hillel trusts his own instincts, makes a decision that this prospective Jew can be taught, and makes a strategy for how to deal with him. What does he do? He writes down the letters of the Hebrew alphabet and starts to teach the *nochri* how to read them. The next day he teaches him the same letters but in the opposite order. When the *nochri* questions him, Hillel tells him that he must trust people if he wants access to the written Torah. He explains that by learning together, the prospective Jew will learn how dependent he is on human interpretation and thus be helped on his journey.

In the third story Shammai seems to be responding in a very logical and appropriate way, because he knows that a proselyte can't possibly become the High Priest and it would be misleading to accept him on this basis. So he sends him away. Hillel, however, accepts him, which seems rather prob-lematic and manipulative because Hillel too knows that the *nochri* can't become the High Priest. But Hillel is, once again, looking at the prospective Jew and considering who he is. He realizes that this person is honest and is being very clear about what he wants – namely, to be the High Priest. So Hillel builds a didactic method based on this honesty; he sends the *nochri* to learn about the laws of the Temple, knowing that he will figure it all out for himself, which is exactly what he does.

In the second story of the non-Jew who is looking for a speedy conversion, Shammai's rejection again seems under-standable. Hillel, however, looks at the *nochri*, but this time it isn't clear quite who he is; Hillel doesn't know if he is coming from a place of honest curiosity, looking to understand the essence of Torah, or if he is taunting him, as Shammai suspected. Hillel's ambivalence results in two versions of this story, found in different printed versions of the Talmud: in one, Hillel accepts him, and in the other, Hillel sends him off to learn, so that he can figure out who the non-Jew really is and what he is really asking.

For me this series of stories presents two distinct approaches to education. Shammai's approach is that of a teacher. He is always concerned with identifying the truth, and so he always asks himself what is the "correct" answer to the question? Therefore, in these stories he is concerned with presenting the truth and controlling the teaching process. Hillel, on the other hand, is an educator. He asks himself, "who is asking the question?" He is interested, first and foremost, in the people, in opening the doors, and in listening carefully in order to identify the motivations and needs of the person standing before him. What is the most appropriate way to engage the learner? Shammai's approach imparts information; Hillel's transforms the learner. This is the difference between teaching and educating. While both approaches have their advantages and disadvantages, it is probably clear by now that I favor Hillel's approach (after all, I worked for the organization that bears his name!). It also seems that the Talmud agrees with me. The stories end by telling us that the three converts met at some point and collectively declared that Shammai's approach had driven them from the world, but Hillel's gentleness and patience brought them under the wings of the divine presence. That is good education: listening to the needs of the individuals and looking for ways to engage them to make an enduring commitment to the future of the Jewish People.

# 13

## Experiments in Jewish Peoplehood

*"Guys, hold your wallets! Infeld has just walked in!" Over the course of my career in leading institutions I spent a lot of time fundraising, and I heard that statement several times. At a farewell event from Hillel, one major donor joked: "I don't understand why we are here celebrating a guy who has dedicated his entire life to making us poorer!" And I honestly thought that I was just a Jewish educator!*

Of course, the donor knew that I wasn't really trying to make him poorer; I was trying to make him a partner in something bigger, helping him use his money to benefit the Jewish People. It turns out that experimenting in Jewish Peoplehood requires educational, leadership, and fundraising skills – often all at the same time.

I am fortunate to have been involved throughout my career in many exciting experiments in Jewish Peoplehood in diverse roles ranging from leader and project coordinator to board member, fundraiser, and more. Whether I was a leader and active participant or merely a spectator on the sidelines, I have watched powerful ideas and successful leaders make changes and contribute to the strengthening of the Jewish People. By reflecting on these experiments – some conscious attempts at Peoplehood education, others unaware of the undertaking – I have extracted several principles and practices that have been repeated time after time and that offer lessons and blueprints for future generations of experimenting Jewish leaders and institutions.

## Core Principles for Experimenting in Jewish Peoplehood

These are the lessons I have learned and tried to implement in the organizations and projects with which I have been most closely involved. The principles come first and are then followed by real examples from my personal experience.

### Listen for opportunity

It is critical to pay close attention to emerging trends and the winds of change and opportunity. This is what I call selective eavesdropping, and it includes a need to be nimble and take risks, responding to the needs of the day, in particular the rapidly changing needs of our contemporary world.

### The power of language

The power of deliberately chosen and well-articulated language to change reality and shape the future should never be underestimated. Language is therefore central to the teaching of Jewish Peoplehood. As I have emphasized in earlier chapters of this book, referring to the process of joining the Jewish family as "conversion" and Jews by choice as "converts" fundamentally misrepresents what is going on and should be replaced by the language of "adoption."

The effective power of language can be seen in the recent decision by the leadership of Beit Hatefutsot to change its English name from the Diaspora Museum to the Museum of the Jewish People. This change of name has redefined everything about the institution. No longer conceived or presented as the memorial to a dying Jewish Diaspora, it has now become the hub for the history and memory of the entire Jewish People, and this has impacted its architecture, programs, and overall mission. I regard this as probably one of the most important acts of transformation in Peoplehood education of the last decade.

## Think big and scale up

In order to take a good idea and scale it to impact the entire Jewish People – or even the world – it is critical to have a big vision and a bold plan, and the past 20 years have seen several examples of successful scaling based on bold initiatives. One is the Diller Teen Fellowship, which has created a replicable model for teen leadership across the globe. Another is Limmud, the incredible transgenerational and transdenominational learning festival that has become one of the most successful Jewish Peoplehood projects, despite having never explicitly put the word "peoplehood" at its center. The vision and tireless energy with which its founders and volunteers have led the adaptation of Limmud in communities throughout the world is a textbook model of global Jewish scaling. Each Limmud event has its own character and reflects the culture of the local Jewish community, but they all follow the same basic principles of volunteerism and non-coercive, pluralistic Jewish learning.

Similarly, several years ago, with the completion of the Reut Institute's research on *Tikkun Olam*, Reut began its Tikkun Olam Makers (TOM) project with its daring goal of finding affordable technological solutions for people with disabilities and impacting millions of people all over the world. I thought it a worthy but unrealistic project. However, within a few short years, TOM hackathons have taken place in cities as diverse as Nazareth, Ho Chi Minh City, San Francisco, and Sao Paolo, and amazing new solutions are being developed.

Even more recently Honeymoon Israel has emerged as a new effort to bring young couples on the periphery of Jewish life to Israel, to experience Jewish Peoplehood and community. In a very short time Honeymoon Israel has built a replicable model that can scale easily and is spreading from city to city.

### Orchestrate the encounter

As discussed previously, a meaningful and deliberate encounter with the "other" has enormous potential as a moment of education and has proved itself more times than I can count. The best experiments in peoplehood create a space for people from different backgrounds to meet, talk, and share experiences. In 1968 I was teaching an evening class twice a week at Ulpan Akiva. It was a Hebrew class for English-speaking immigrant women, and we taught them children's stories, so that they could keep up with what their children were learning at school. At the same time, another evening class was taking place for North African immigrant women, most of whom were totally illiterate. They already knew lots of stories and songs in Hebrew, but they couldn't read or write in any language and were being taught how to read. I made sure that during the evening there was a 50-minute break at the same time for everyone and, amazingly, just as I had hoped, these women from such different backgrounds found that they actually had a lot in common and bonded incredibly well. It was the whole point of the evening and one of the most exciting Jewish educational experiences of my entire life.

### The importance of people

Central to every lesson in this book are the people: my teachers and mentors, my colleagues and partners, donors, staff, students, and others. There is no way to build the Jewish People without recognizing the power of people in every effort; this is true when building a team, galvanizing support, or raising money. I have always believed in listening to the people around me, learning from them, and building relationships with them.

### *Serve the Jewish People – not just your members*

Every organization to which I have devoted significant energy has had an inclusive approach to its target population. I have always been drawn to transdenominational and transgenerational organizations with the potential to impact all Jews and not just members of a particular sub-group or denomination. Peoplehood efforts must focus on the whole People, maximizing diversity as much as possible.

## Melitz

Melitz, the organization I founded and ran for over 30 years, expressed all of these principles in different ways. It started with the deliberate choice of name. Many believe that Melitz took its name from the Hebrew acronym for Institutes for Jewish Zionist Education, which is only partly true. I chose the name because of the story in the Book of Genesis about Joseph and his brothers. In the part of the story where Joseph is the viceroy of Egypt and the brothers come seeking food, the Torah says that the brothers didn't realize that Joseph (whom they didn't recognize) actually understood them because "the *melitz* was amongst them" (Genesis 42:23). In other words, there was a *melitz* present to help interpret the conversation. A *melitz* functions to help siblings who have taken different directions in life understand each other and communicate. Perfect! That is what Melitz was all about. It was never in the business of making the siblings resemble each other or changing their pathways; the goal was to connect them so they could understand each other.

Having a diverse staff was particularly important at Mel-

itz, and it was no accident that the core team included gradu-
ates of different rabbinical seminaries, a settler from the West
Bank, a university professor, immigrants from different parts
of the world, native-born Israelis, a high-school principal from
the kibbutz movement, and many others. I knew that I had to
build Melitz and its staff so that any Jew could identify with
at least one of them. Every member of the diverse team offered
something unique and complemented my strengths. They were
all better than me in their individual fields, but I knew enough
about what each of them did to negotiate with them all and
bring them together.

One Saturday night I was driving home from a lecture I
had given in Jerusalem near the old train station. There was a
clash between two opposing demonstrations: Peace Now and
Gush Emunim, the settlers' movement. There was terrible traf-
fic and no way through. The leaders of both demonstrations
were members of the Melitz staff, and they let me through
right away. I was so proud that they were both able to work pro-
fessionally with people they would later demonstrate against.
The multiple perspectives of the team were so different, each
with their own point of view and approach, and we therefore
produced outstanding materials on a wide variety of topics.

We also adapted our activities in response to changing
needs and opportunities in the Jewish world. In the early years,
I was on a plane from Israel to South Africa, and there was a
group of Christians who had been touring Israel. In talking
to them about their trip it became clear that they had no idea
that they had been in a Jewish state; their experience was of the
Holy Land! They hadn't met any Jews and had no understanding of Jews as we understand ourselves. Finding this intolera-
ble, we opened Melitz's Center for Christian Encounter with
Israel. We worked with many groups of Christians over the
years and were honored to receive an award from the Queen
for our work with the UK's Council for Christians and Jews.

A similar moment of opportunity presented itself in the 1990s when the Soviet Union collapsed and hundreds of thousands of Russians started arriving in Israel. We saw a need and met it by opening a Russian-speaking department, which was headed by the current speaker of the Knesset, Yuli Edelstein. Melitz started to produce Jewish educational materials to help those cut off from the Jewish People for decades renew their connection to Jewish memory. Among the things that we produced to send into the (Former) Soviet Union was a series of videos teaching Jewish history. They were made as news broadcasts showing Jewish historical events. There was the Exodus from Egypt, for example, with reporters talking about the plagues and reporting on the plans of the Israelites to leave. There were lots of immigrant families arriving in Israel at that time, and the government had a plan to match immigrant families with veteran Israelis, so no family would be alone during the *Pesach* (Passover) holiday. We too adopted a family. They came to us for the *seder*; they didn't know a word of Hebrew or English, and we didn't speak Russian. While we were waiting for my Russian-speaking mother to arrive, I showed them the video that we had created at Melitz. As they were watching they got very upset. They thought the news was real and happening right then!

### Taglit Birthright Israel

Taglit Birthright Israel is one of the boldest and most innovative Jewish programs of recent times. It was born from a vision to impact the whole Jewish People and has revolutionized Jewish education and trips to Israel. Taglit Birthright Israel was developed by diverse Israeli and American teams. In Israel, Yossi Beilin (the original innovator) had a team working on the models and structure for the program. I had been hired to run the planning for the program, and when I met with

Beilin's team, I was delighted to discover that it was led by Gidi Grinstein, a young Israeli I had met years before. The team was an amazing group of highly intelligent young people who excelled in technology and systems management. Even though I was their boss, I soon became their pupil and learned so much from them. It was immediately clear that it was crazy that a group of Israelis was building something that should be an international Jewish project without input from Diaspora Jews. So I flew to America where I met with Jeffrey Solomon from the Andrea and Charles Bronfman Philanthropies, and he took me to McKinsey, where they gave us a pro-bono team to think about what Birthright should be. I took both teams and merged them; the Israelis and the Diaspora Jews put their various perspectives together and did amazing work. The principles that guide Taglit Birthright Israel today were developed in that team, a team which I officially ran but which was actually a learning experience for me unlike any other.

## Hillel: The Foundation for Jewish Campus Life

In August 2000 I was invited by Richard Joel, then president of Hillel, the international Jewish student organization, to lecture at the annual retreat for Hillel professionals. Little did I know then that this would eventually lead to me becoming president of Hillel, one of the highlights of my career. That invitation was my first reconnection with Hillel in over 30 years, and my expectations were low. The Hillel chapters I was familiar with from my time as a *shaliach* in Baltimore provided committed Jewish students with Jewish services on campus, such as kosher food and prayer services. Yet the language I heard at that retreat seemed to come from another planet! They were talking about "engagement," "doing Jewish with other Jews," and the "global Jewish People." Here was a large organization using language and values on an international scale. And they were doing it with a pluralistic and Peoplehood-focused approach. For example, there was the principle that at every Hillel event there would be multiple prayer service options and each denomination could decide what time their services would begin, but they all had to end at precisely the same time. What an amazing sight it was to watch Jewish students all leave their different prayer services, mingling as they walked together to a single dining facility where they ate, sang, spoke, and danced as one Jewish People.

I very much wanted to be a part of this exciting movement and therefore did not hesitate to accept Richard's offer that I serve as consul for Jewish affairs. This entailed spending 70 days a year visiting campuses and talking to students, professionals, academics, and lay boards about the Jewish People. When Richard Joel left Hillel for Yeshiva University, I was asked to succeed him as president.

Hillel was (and remains) unique in being transdenominational and global, with Israel and *Tikkun Olam* as core values through which it models being "distinctively Jewish and universally human." It also scaled successfully by exporting and adapting its programs to major Jewish centers throughout the world, including the FSU, Eastern Europe, South America, and, of course, Israel. After all, the only thing that over 80% of Jews do today is go to college, and so it is the sensible place to be if we really want to ensure the continued significant renaissance of the Jewish People.

## New Horizons for Jewish Peoplehood

In addition to all the successful examples already mentioned, there is, undoubtedly, room for more and better experiments in Jewish Peoplehood. An institution that has, in my opinion, the potential to make a significant but as yet unrealized contribution to the advancement of Jewish Peoplehood is the Jewish

Community Center (JCC). JCCs are, by their nature, transgenerational and transdenominational and do not claim to provide specific answers for how Jewish life should look; instead they can concentrate on provoking and enabling the questions vital to Jewish education. When we walk into a synagogue, we are automatically defined as different from other types of Jews. At a JCC, on the other hand, we can demonstrate our belonging to the entire Jewish People despite our denominational differences. It is this unique combination of attributes that has not been fully recognized or exploited in North America in contrast to Europe where there are JCCs that see themselves as serving the whole community, according to the vision of Rabbi Mordechai Kaplan. I believe it is imperative for the future of Jewish Peoplehood that the JCCs in North America are strengthened to serve the entire Jewish community and not only JCC members.

There is also great potential in the emerging gap year programs for young adults. While gap year programs bringing Diaspora Jews to Israel have been running successfully for at least 30 years, there are new and flourishing pre-army programs in Israel (*mechinot*) attracting Israeli youngsters for a year of study or volunteer work. Some of these, Kol Ami for example, bring Israelis and Diaspora Jews together, and such programs could have a great impact on the Jewish future. I believe these programs should be expanded and developed to expose all young Jews to each other for powerful moments of education.

## Philanthropy and Fundraising

Every single one of the aforementioned organizations and programs depend in large part on the commitment of generous philanthropists who want to use their money for the greater good. These people are without a doubt the life support system that enables dreams to become realities. Over the years I have known philanthropists who support activities for very different reasons. Some are mission driven and seek out institutions with particular values and missions. Some are excited to support good ideas that they hadn't planned in advance and others are motivated by the relationship that they have developed with a Jewish institutional leader. There are those who rarely say no but never make long-term commitments and then there are the philanthropic dynasties. These are the families who have built philanthropy into the culture of their families and who have educated their offspring to continue the tradition of giving. For them, it is not the thrill of giving that excites, but the recognition of their responsibility to make important things happen. Recently I received a grant from a family foundation that I have been connected to for over fifty years. The family members now in charge are the fourth generation that I have known and worked with.

While there are those who find asking for money intimidating, I have never been shy or reticent, because I see it as a privilege to offer these generous people the opportunity to partner in building the Jewish People.

For me, fundraising is all about the people and the relationships to be built with them. I had, for example, a good relationship with a prominent community leader and donor I met during my *shlichut*. Many years later I heard he was in Jerusalem, called him up, and asked him to have dinner with me. We had a lovely dinner and at the end he said to me: "Nu, what do you want to ask for?" "I don't want anything," I replied, "I simply wanted to see you and have dinner." And it was true; I had no ulterior motive. Yet, he was shocked that someone would want to have dinner with him without asking him for money. I guess being a philanthropist can sometimes be a lonely experience.

I learned a lot about fundraising from my mentor, Rabbi David Hartman, who would always invite his potential donors to learn Torah with him. He offered them something meaningful so that they too were gaining. "Never begin with the money," he told me. I also learned not to gain anything personally from the gifts I raised; the benefits must go only to the donors themselves and the organization that is going to do the work.

Even though most of my career has involved raising the money so that the Jewish education could happen, a few years ago I was given the opportunity to work for the Chais Family Foundation and give away money for the first time. I discovered that it is almost as difficult to give away money as it is to raise it. So many questions arise: How do you judge what is worthy? What is the best way to make the changes you want to make? It was a very important lesson for me to sit on the other side of the table, and I am very grateful for that opportunity. I was often told by potential grantees that the conversations I had with them were different than with other funders because they knew that I had been one of them and asked different questions.

## Being Grateful for Our Blessings

We are living in a unique time: we have witnessed the end of the Soviet Union, we have a strong State of Israel, and there are no more Jewish refugees. The Jewish People has so much potential. It is time for even more experiments in the renaissance of the Jewish People that combine daring and bold visions with the best educational methodologies and the support of committed philanthropists.

# *Part 3*

## The Future of the Jewish People

# 14

## Future Challenges and Directions

The Jewish People today face many challenges that require strong leadership and creative approaches. Just like the era in which the automobile was created, a change of attitude is necessary. In those days people who thought they were in the business of horses and wagons went out of business. However, those who realized that they were in the business of transportation found a way to adapt to the new reality. The Jewish People must do the same. Despite the challenges of the last half-century and the issues that we face today, I believe that we are living in a unique time with an incredible opportunity to contribute to the significant renaissance of the Jewish People. Rebirth is constant; it doesn't stop. There is so much to do, and what a time to be doing it!

In 1945, when the war ended, the Jewish People were at an extremely low point. Yet today, just a few generations later, there has been a revolution in Jewish life. Who would have thought then that by the early years of the twenty-first century we would be in such a position? We have a strong state; there are more people learning Torah than ever before; and there is such vibrancy and experimentation in Jewish life.

In this time of growth and change, now is the time for strong and inspired leadership. One of the most important roles of a leader is to anticipate the imminent challenges and lead the community in dealing with them. As we look to the future and I pass on my lessons to the next generation, I offer my recipe for dealing with the challenges and directions that leaders must, in my opinion, take to secure our future well-being.

Bearing in mind what the Jewish People have been through and the fact that we are living in a post-Emancipation world which is becoming more and more diverse and global, I see the following as the central challenges facing us today and in the near future: maintaining unity without requiring uniformity; ensuring that Israel remains the nation-state of the whole Jewish People; reorienting Jewish institutions so that they recognize their shared mission and respect their different tasks; addressing the challenge of intermarriage and assimilation; and fulfilling our unique purpose in the world.

Below are my prescriptions for dealing with each of these issues.

# A.

## Ensuring Unity Without Uniformity –
## The Model of the 5 Legged Table

The model of the 5 Legged Table deals with the fractured nature of Jewish identity today and reflects my deep desire for us to remain unified rather than uniform. It is an approach to Jewish identity and peoplehood that offers a recipe for how Jews can be active members of the Jewish People in today's world.

The five "legs" of the 5 Legged Table are: Memory, Family, Mount Sinai, Israel, and Hebrew. These are the components or building blocks that, for me, encompass Jewish identity and all of Jewish life. In the course of building a Jewish life and identity, a person should ideally relate to all five legs and consider which they find meaningful and can express in action. Like any table, the more legs it has, the more stable it will be; so a Jewish identity composed of all five components will be strong and flourishing. However, if a person finds that they can relate to only three legs, it is still possible to maintain the table, as three legs are enough for stability. But with less than three legs, the table cannot stand; so too a Jewish identity built on only one or two legs is not rich enough to sustain itself. Not only is the table unstable with two legs, more importantly, unity will also be lost. This is due to the magic of the number five. If every Jew commits to a minimum of three of the five legs, they will automatically have something in common with other Jews, enough to create a strong and thriving Jewish future. There will be unity – we will be building our collective identities on the same principles – but without requiring uniformity.

The 5 Legged Table is a framework that values personal choice in which a person can decide on the elements that make the most sense for them and still remain within the broader framework of the Jewish People. It allows each person to choose as an individual what from the past they can take into the future and make an integral part of their lives – but as part of something bigger, namely, the Jewish People. It allows all of us to eat from the same pot of *tsimmes* but gives us some options for choosing our own seasonings.

The core ideas for the five legs of Jewish identity appear in detail in the chapters of Part I as components of Jewish Peoplehood, but I summarize them here briefly.

### Memory

There is no verb that appears in Jewish culture more than the verb *zakhor*, to remember. Our collective memories provide us with the values, beliefs, and rituals that are the foundation of our shared peoplehood. They remind us where we came from and instruct us how to behave. We break a glass at a wedding to remind us of the destruction of the Temple; when we sit down to a Passover *seder*, year after year and all over the world, we reanimate our collective memory through the songs, stories, and rituals of the *seder*. Memory is activated through education and by learning and participating in the rituals that embody the memories and the stories of our culture. Jews have memory, not history.

## Family

Whose memories are they? They are ours, and we are the Jewish family. From the early familial roots of the children of Israel, the Jewish People expanded into a much larger extended family, no longer bound by immediate genealogical ties but maintaining strong tribal bonds nonetheless. Being part of the Jewish People means having an ever shifting sense of belonging, from the small family to the bigger tribe and back again, and belonging to a family means having connections and being responsible for other members of the family, even the most distant cousins, and a commitment to its continued significant future.

## Mount Sinai

This leg relates to what happened to the Jewish People on their journey from slavery in Egypt to the Land of Israel; to the moment when they stopped in the desert and something crucial happened. Whether or not it really happened, this event changed us forever. Mount Sinai signifies the earliest recognition of a transcendent power and the ensuing realization that if there is already a God, then human beings are *not* God. While we may strive to imitate God, we must never believe that we are God, because if (or when) we do, terrible things ensue.

The idea of Mount Sinai goes on to include the covenant between God and the Jewish People, where we received the Torah in both written and oral form. From here we learn the values and rituals that are our particular inheritance and that govern our behaviors, our role in the world, and our contribution to humanity. It was at Mount Sinai that the Jewish People printed its visiting card.

## The Land and State of Israel

The Jewish family has a homeland: its eternal destination and its historical home. Every single inch of the Land of Israel is a warehouse of Jewish collective memory. It is also the place where the laws of modern nationalism were activated in order to create a state, and is the only place where the Jewish People are attempting to put Jewish values into action as a majority people with full power over their destiny and self-identity. The Jewish State has ensured that there will never be another Jewish refugee with nowhere to go, and even for those who choose to settle elsewhere, Israel is still the place where the Jewish People can express their national identity. While Jews may have individual homes anywhere, Israel is the only place that is a home to all Jews.

## Hebrew

Language is not only a means of communication, it is also a way of transferring culture across generations. The Hebrew language not only unites Jews from all over the world in the present, it also provides access to the Jewish past. Hebrew is our shared language, embodying our values, our memories, and our aspirations for the future. Hebrew expresses a particular way of being in the world, and when Jews cannot access their language, they are shut out of the long-running Jewish conversation. While we do not imagine all Jews will become conversant in modern Hebrew, the inclusion of Hebrew words and phrases with their inherent values is essential to the Jewish future.

### The 5 Legged Table

I have shared the model of the 5 Legged Table with tens of thousands of Jews all over the world. The conversations that I have had with some of them and the curricula and educational programs that have been initiated on the basis of the model have convinced me of its usefulness and relevance. I continue to engage with the educational question of how to encourage and sustain an educational system that teaches all five legs and enables and legitimizes the choice of any three. It is my hope that this book, together with the ongoing work of Melitz, will continue to catalyze discussion and ideas around this question and the model, so that the Jewish People can meet the challenge of being unified without being uniform.

# B.

## Ensuring that Israel Remains the Nation-State of the Jewish People

In recent years I have been involved in the Reut Institute's efforts to research and consider how Israel can remain the nation-state of the whole Jewish People. Our work has produced clear evidence of the extent to which a widening gap has developed between Israel's aspirations to be the nation-state of the Jewish People and the emerging reality that constantly challenges this aspiration.

Fifty years ago, after the Six Day War, when I was the community *shaliach* in Baltimore, Jews of different denominations suddenly felt united by their shared connection to Israel and started working and celebrating together. The local Jewish institutions grew dramatically, there were parades and celebrations, and Israel was a unifying force for the whole Jewish community. However, when I returned recently to Baltimore to teach, I discovered that Israel has become the most divisive issue in Jewish life today and not just in Baltimore. Supporting Israel has too often become identified with partisan politics and religious extremism. Leadership in the Diaspora and in Israel struggle to distinguish between criticism of some of Israel's policies and hardline opposition to Israel's very right to exist. Not only this, but many fear that the Israeli establishment has given up on the rest of North American Jewry, both as supporters of Israel and also as Jews, whose wellbeing, once the *raison d'être* of the state, is no longer of Israel's supreme concern.

Yet Israel's relationship with world Jewry is not only a Zionist imperative, it is also of deep strategic importance. It was Israel as the homeland of the Jewish People that was granted international recognition by the United Nations and all Western and many other countries, and it is only as such that it can retain legitimacy.

Strong and committed leadership in both Israel and the Diaspora is critical to ensure that the State and the Land of Israel remain core elements of Jewish collective identity. Israeli and Diaspora leaders are both responsible for ensuring that: Jewish education enables individual Jews to link their personal memory to the collective memory of the Jewish People; Hebrew is not only a language of prayer but the conveyor of central cultural values from one generation to another; Israel is far more than just a political entity in the Middle East or their grandparents' favorite charity; "your People is my People" precedes "your God is my God"; we learn to *love* an Israel that at any particular moment we may struggle to *like*; and Judaism is not a religion but the religious culture of the Jewish People in whatever form Jewish institutions choose to define it.

I believe that we have to make a distinction between our love for the Land of Israel and our need for the State of Israel. As I have already said, the Land of Israel is the place where the Jewish People is indigenous, and it is the warehouse of Jewish memories. These should not be used as political statements, however, and the political questions facing the State of Israel need to be analyzed using other means and in other terms. They should be determined by considerations of security, diplomacy, and sustainability and not of religion, memory, or history, and they must take into account moral values and our standing in the world. I want Israel to be a source of respect and values that can guide and lead other peoples, but there is no way that the Jewish People can succeed in leading in the area of *Tikkun Olam*, as I believe it must, when the State of Israel is occupying another people. We must take care of this issue first, and only then will we be free to make the contribution to the world that we were commanded to make.

In addition, I believe that leadership in both communities must work toward achieving the following mutual understandings:

- Israel must remain a democracy that leaves final decision making in the hands of its citizens;

- All Israel's citizens, whether Jewish or not, must be equal under the law with full and equal social, political, and civil rights;

- Freedom of religion as promised in Israel's Declaration of Independence must be applied to members of the Jewish People as well so that no religious denomination has the right to impose its definitions on any others.

We may be on the brink of a chasm that will divide us

beyond repair, but joint leadership in Israel and the Diaspora still hold in their hands the means, the institutions, and the opportunity to ensure that Israel remains the nation-state of the entire Jewish People.

# C.

## Re-Engineering the Infrastructure of the Jewish People: One Mission, Many Tasks

Often when I talk to Jewish organizational leaders about making changes and doing new things, they tell me to wait until they have finished revising their mission statement! How can that be? In the world today there can only be one mission a Jewish organization can possibly have – namely how to ensure the continued significant renaissance of the Jewish People. That is the core mission of the Jewish People everywhere, and I believe that everyone shares this mission: the rabbis, the nursery school teachers, the Israeli prime minister, all community institutions. That mission is why we created a state, why we build synagogues, and schools, and why we need Federations. Community leaders need to reconstruct their Jewish communities to make it clear that different institutions have different tasks within this shared mission. Rabbis, for example, have a particular task in our mission. Jewish education plays a very important role, as do the JCCs. None of them should be competing with each other for the best or most important mission. We need to move away from debating our mission statements and get on with our complementary tasks. Imagine how it would be if each institution carried out its task secure in the knowledge that it was playing its unique part in achieving a joint mission. If I had a single message to the prime minister of Israel, the kindergarten teacher, the Hillel professional, and all the Jewish institutions out there, it would be to remind them that they have something in common – namely, a mission to continue the significant renaissance of the Jewish People, and that they are responsible for accomplishing that mission to the best of their ability. When we are aware that we share a mission with other institutions, we recognize the complementary roles we all play, find ways to work in an atmosphere of mutual respect, and neutralize the competition. There are no more fights over territory, because we respect the other institutions that are doing their part to contribute to the shared mission. It is therefore the role of strong leaders today to bring institutions together with a single purpose and unique tasks.

# D.

## Must Intermarriage Be Synonymous with Assimilation?

For my great-grandmother, intermarriage was not an issue; she had probably never met a non-Jew. For my grandmother, it was an issue; for my mother, it was a tragedy; for me, it is a fact of life. Intermarriage is a challenge for the Jewish family and affects almost every part of the Jewish world. There may be no way to stop it at this point, but I am hopeful that we can still create a situation in which intermarriage is not necessarily assimilation. I am vehemently against assimilation, and I believe that we can fight it by engaging "interfaith" couples and families with the five "legs" of Jewish identity, so they can choose how to build a life of belonging to the Jewish family. The word "interfaith" works in a world where Judaism is understood as a religion. However, when we deal with this issue through the prism of Judaism as a family or a people – my preferred approach – the language is about joining the family. This gives us a positive and productive way to adopt new members into the family, to help them acquire the memories they need, and to contribute in a meaningful way. It does not demand that adoption is unconditional, but it does demand that adoption takes place in the spirit of welcoming. Maybe we could create a new status for the non-Jewish partner in a Jewish family. There is even a precedent for this in Jewish tradition; we call it *"ger toshav."*

The question that we must ask is, what are the frameworks for adoption and the requirements for the new family member that will prevent assimilation? From my experience with educational initiatives for these families, I have seen how the power of community can help them feel welcomed into the Jewish family and how Shabbat and holiday celebrations give them concrete and accessible ways to connect. I have also been surprised to see how learning Hebrew can be an empowering and motivating force for them. Given that I see Hebrew as one of the five "legs" of Jewish identity, perhaps I shouldn't be so surprised! Whatever the method, however, I believe that the Jewish community has an imperative to find ways to invite these new members of the family to bind their future to ours for the benefit of the whole collective.

# E.

## Fulfilling Our True Mission: *Tikkun Olam*

Israeli and Diaspora Jews today have no common project to unite them. There is so little (if anything) that we do together; our worlds and interests are so different. Our relationship sometimes reminds me of an empty-nester couple who, after years of raising their children together, are left with no common core and begin to question why they share a bed. We, the entire Jewish People, need to find something to keep us together.

In the past we won many battles together as the whole Jewish People; we took Jews out of Yemen, out of Syria, and out of the Soviet Union. We built a state. These were all shared projects that Israeli and Diaspora Jews worked on together. Today, these problems have, thankfully, been solved, and we are left with nothing to tie us all together, not even the State of Israel.

*Tikkun Olam*, the concept of repairing the world, is, I believe, an issue around which Jews from all over the world can unite. It returns us to the Jewish People's first conversation with God, where He told us: "Build a family, go to your Land and may all families on earth be blessed by your presence." In the past decades, following the Holocaust, we found the strength to follow the first two commands. Now we have to relate to the last with equal commitment and ensure that the world can be blessed by our presence.

*Tikkun Olam* answers our need to give meaning to our lives, but there is currently much confusion about what *Tikkun Olam* actually is. It is far more than making sandwiches for homeless people or volunteering at a retirement home. While these actions are certainly worthy and may even be *mitzvot*, they are not powerful or far-reaching enough to stimulate a joint project between Israeli and Diaspora Jews. *Tikkun Olam*, on the other hand, is systematic, strategic, and far-reaching and creates new ways that the Jewish People can work together to fix the evils of the world.

I have a dream that one day the Jewish People will receive the Nobel Prize for *Tikkun Olam*! Is there any point in being Jewish without aiming to improve the world? None of the other things we do as Jews have ultimate purpose; the only thing that gives us that ultimate purpose is looking outward to make a difference in the world. God created an incomplete world, and it is our job to complete it. I call on the leadership of the Jewish world, in Israel and beyond, to promote and strengthen the opportunities for Jews to be involved jointly in *Tikkun Olam*, in the name of and involving the entire Jewish People.

In Yehuda Avner's wonderful book *The Prime Ministers* he describes Golda Meir's appointment as Israel's foreign minister in 1956. Avner quotes a speech that she gave at the time in which she declared her intention to work with African and Asian countries. Meir believed it was the role of the Jewish State to help the poorer nations of the world. She wanted to do *Tikkun Olam* in the name of the Jewish People, and she is the inspiration for my belief that the Jewish People today need to unite around a common project to fulfill the blessing that "the nations of the world shall be blessed through you."

# Appendix A

## The Declaration of the State of Israel

ERETZ-ISRAEL [ארץ ישראל – the Land of Israel, Palestine] was the birthplace of the Jewish people. Here their spiritual, religious and political identity was shaped. Here they first attained to statehood, created cultural values of national and universal significance and gave to the world the eternal Book of Books.

After being forcibly exiled from their land, the people kept faith with it throughout their Dispersion and never ceased to pray and hope for their return to it and for the restoration in it of their political freedom.

Impelled by this historic and traditional attachment, Jews strove in every successive generation to re-establish themselves in their ancient homeland. In recent decades they returned in their masses. Pioneers, *ma'pilim* [מעפילים – immigrants coming to Eretz-Israel in defiance of restrictive legislation] and defenders, they made deserts bloom, revived the Hebrew language, built villages and towns, and created a thriving community controlling its own economy and culture, loving peace but knowing how to defend itself, bringing the blessings of progress to all the country's inhabitants, and aspiring towards independent nationhood.

In the year 5657 (1897), at the summons of the
spiritual father of the Jewish State, Theodore Herzl,
the First Zionist Congress convened and proclaimed
the right of the Jewish people to national rebirth in
its own country.

This right was recognized in the Balfour Declaration
of the 2nd November, 1917, and re-affirmed in
the Mandate of the League of Nations which, in
particular, gave international sanction to the historic
connection between the Jewish people and Eretz-
Israel and to the right of the Jewish people to rebuild
its National Home.

The catastrophe which recently befell the Jewish
people – the massacre of millions of Jews in Europe
– was another clear demonstration of the urgency
of solving the problem of its homelessness by re-
establishing in Eretz-Israel the Jewish State, which
would open the gates of the homeland wide to every
Jew and confer upon the Jewish people the status of a
fully privileged member of the comity of nations.

Survivors of the Nazi holocaust in Europe, as well
as Jews from other parts of the world, continued to
migrate to Eretz-Israel, undaunted by difficulties,
restrictions and dangers, and never ceased to assert
their right to a life of dignity, freedom and honest toil
in their national homeland.

In the Second World War, the Jewish community of
this country contributed its full share to the struggle
of the freedom – and peace-loving nations against
the forces of Nazi wickedness and, by the blood of

its soldiers and its war effort, gained the right to be reckoned among the peoples who founded the United Nations.

On the 29th November, 1947, the United Nations General Assembly passed a resolution calling for the establishment of a Jewish State in Eretz-Israel; the General Assembly required the inhabitants of Eretz-Israel to take such steps as were necessary on their part for the implementation of that resolution. This recognition by the United Nations of the right of the Jewish people to establish their State is irrevocable.

This right is the natural right of the Jewish people to be masters of their own fate, like all other nations, in their own sovereign State.

ACCORDINGLY WE, MEMBERS OF THE PEOPLE'S COUNCIL, REPRESENTATIVES OF THE JEWISH COMMUNITY OF ERETZ-ISRAEL AND OF THE ZIONIST MOVEMENT, ARE HERE ASSEMBLED ON THE DAY OF THE TERMINATION OF THE BRITISH MANDATE OVER ERETZ-ISRAEL AND, BY VIRTUE OF OUR NATURAL AND HISTORIC RIGHT AND ON THE STRENGTH OF THE RESOLUTION OF THE UNITED NATIONS GENERAL ASSEMBLY, HEREBY DECLARE THE ESTABLISHMENT OF A JEWISH STATE IN ERETZ-ISRAEL, TO BE KNOWN AS THE STATE OF ISRAEL.

WE DECLARE that, with effect from the moment of the termination of the Mandate being tonight, the eve of Sabbath, the 6th Iyar, 5708 (15th May, 1948), until the establishment of the elected, regular authorities of the State in accordance with the Constitution which shall be adopted by the Elected Constituent Assembly not later than the 1st October 1948, the People's Council shall act as a Provisional Council of State, and its executive organ, the People's Administration, shall be the Provisional Government of the Jewish State, to be called "Israel".

THE STATE OF ISRAEL will be open for Jewish immigration and for the Ingathering of the Exiles; it will foster the development of the country for the benefit of all its inhabitants; it will be based on freedom, justice and peace as envisaged by the prophets of Israel; it will ensure complete equality of social and political rights to all its inhabitants irrespective of religion, race or sex; it will guarantee freedom of religion, conscience, language, education and culture; it will safeguard the Holy Places of all religions; and it will be faithful to the principles of the Charter of the United Nations.

THE STATE OF ISRAEL is prepared to cooperate with the agencies and representatives of the United Nations in implementing the resolution of the General Assembly of the 29th November, 1947, and will take steps to bring about the economic union of the whole of Eretz-Israel.

WE APPEAL to the United Nations to assist the Jewish people in the building-up of its State and to receive the State of Israel into the comity of nations.

WE APPEAL – in the very midst of the onslaught launched against us now for months – to the Arab inhabitants of the State of Israel to preserve peace and participate in the upbuilding of the State on the basis of full and equal citizenship and due representation in all its provisional and permanent institutions.

WE EXTEND our hand to all neighbouring states and their peoples in an offer of peace and good neighbourliness, and appeal to them to establish bonds of cooperation and mutual help with the sovereign Jewish people settled in its own land. The State of Israel is prepared to do its share in a common effort for the advancement of the entire Middle East.

WE APPEAL to the Jewish people throughout the Diaspora to rally round the Jews of Eretz-Israel in the tasks of immigration and upbuilding and to stand by them in the great struggle for the realization of the age-old dream – the redemption of Israel.

PLACING OUR TRUST IN THE "ROCK OF ISRAEL", WE AFFIX OUR SIGNATURES TO THIS PROCLAMATION AT THIS SESSION OF THE PROVISIONAL COUNCIL OF STATE, ON THE SOIL OF THE HOMELAND, IN THE CITY OF TEL-AVIV, ON THIS SABBATH EVE, THE 5TH DAY OF IYAR, 5708 (14TH MAY, 1948).

# Appendix B

## Shabbat 31a Hillel and Shammai – "On One Foot"

תנו רבנן [אבות דרבי נתן פ״טו
מ״ג]: 'מעשה בנכרי אחד שבא
לפני שמאי, אמר לו: כמה
תורות יש לכם?

אמר לו: שתים, תורה שבכתב
ותורה שבעל פה.

אמר לו: שבכתב אני מאמינך,
ושבעל פה איני מאמינך;
גיירני על מנת שתלמדני תורה
שבכתב!

גער בו והוציאו בנזיפה.

בא לפני הלל, גייריה. יומא
קמא אמר לו: א״ב ג״ד. למחר
אפיך ליה.

אמר לו: והא אתמול לא
אמרת לי הכי?

אמר לו: לאו עלי דידי קא
סמכת? דעל פה נמי סמוך עלי.

שוב מעשה בנכרי אחד שבא
לפני שמאי, אמר לו: גיירני על
מנת שתלמדני כל התורה כולה
כשאני עומד על רגל אחת!

Our Rabbis taught: A certain heathen once came before Shammai and asked him, 'How many Torahs have you?' 'Two,' he replied: 'the Written Torah and the Oral Torah.' 'I believe you with respect to the Written, but not with respect to the Oral Torah; make me a proselyte on condition that you teach me the Written Torah [only]. [But] he scolded and repulsed him in anger. When he went before Hillel, he accepted him as a proselyte. On the first day, he taught him, Alef, beth, gimmel, daleth; the following day he reversed [them ] to him. 'But yesterday you did not teach them to me thus,' he

146

דחפו באמת הבנין שבידו.

בא לפני הלל, גייריה. אמר לו: "דעלך סני – לחברך לא תעביד" – זו היא כל התורה כולה, ואידך פירושה הוא, זיל גמור.

שוב מעשה בנכרי אחד שהיה עובר אחורי בית המדרש ושמע קול סופר שהיה אומר (שמות כח ד) ואלה הבגדים אשר יעשו חושן ואפוד [ומעיל וכתנת תשבץ מצנפת ואבנט ועשו בגדי קדש לאהרן אחיך ולבניו לכהנו לי]; אמר: הללו למי?

אמרו לו: לכהן גדול.

אמר אותו נכרי בעצמו: אלך ואתגייר בשביל שישימוני כהן גדול.

בא לפני שמאי, אמר ליה: גיירני על מנת שתשימני כהן גדול! דחפו באמת הבנין שבידו.

בא לפני הלל, גייריה, אמר לו: כלום מעמידין מלך אלא מי שיודע טכסיסי מלכות? לך למוד טכסיסי מלכות!

הלך וקרא; כיון שהגיע (במדבר א נא) [ובנסע המשכן יורידו אתו הלוים ובחנת המשכן יקימו אתו הלוים] והזר

protested. 'Must you then not rely upon me? Then rely upon me with respect to the Oral [Torah] too.'

On another occasion it happened that a certain heathen came before Shammai and said to him, 'Make me a proselyte, on condition that you teach me the whole Torah while I stand on one foot.' Thereupon he repulsed him with the builder's cubit which was in his hand. When he went before Hillel, he said to him, 'What is hateful to you, do not to your neighbour: that is the whole Torah, while the rest is the commentary thereof; go and learn it.'

On another occasion it happened that a certain heathen was passing behind a Beth Hamidrash, when he heard the voice of a teacher reciting, And these are the garments which they shall make; a breastplate, and an ephod. Said he, 'For whom are these?' 'For the

הקרב יומת, אמר ליה: מקרא
זה על מי נאמר?

אמר לו: אפילו על דוד מלך
ישראל.

נשא אותו גר קל וחומר
בעצמו: ומה ישראל שנקראו
בנים למקום, ומתוך אהבה
שאהבם קרא להם (שמות ד
כב) [ואמרת אל פרעה כה
אמר ה'] בני בכורי ישראל,
כתיב עליהם 'והזר הקרב
יומת', גר, הקל, שבא במקלו
ובתרמילו – על אחת כמה
וכמה!

בא לפני שמאי, אמר לו: כלום
ראוי אני להיות כהן גדול?
והלא כתיב בתורה 'והזר הקרב
יומת'? בא לפני הלל, אמר לו:
ענוותן הלל! ינוחו לך ברכות
על ראשך, שהקרבתני תחת
כנפי השכינה!

High Priest,' he was told. Then said that heathen to himself, 'I will go and become a proselyte, that I may be appointed a High Priest.' So he went before Shammai and said to him, 'Make me a proselyte on condition that you appoint me a High Priest.' But he repulsed him with the builder's cubit which was in his hand. He then went before Hillel, who made him a proselyte. Said he to him, 'Can any man be made a king but he who knows the arts of government? Do you go and study the arts of government!' He went and read. When he came to, "and the stranger that cometh nigh shall be put to death", he asked him, 'To whom does this verse apply?' 'Even to David King of Israel,' was the answer. Thereupon that proselyte reasoned within himself a fortiori: if Israel, who are called sons of the Omnipresent, and who in His love for them He designated them, Israel is my son, my firstborn, yet it is written of them, 'and the stranger that cometh nigh shall be put to death': how much more so a mere proselyte, who comes with his staff and wallet! Then he went before Shammai and said to him. 'Am I then eligible to be a High Priest; is it not written in the Torah, 'and the stranger that cometh nigh shall be put to death?' He went before Hillel and said to him, 'O gentle Hillel; blessings rest on thy head for bringing me under the wings of the Shechinah!'

Some time later the three met in one place; said they, Shammai's impatience sought to drive us from the world, but Hillel's gentleness brought us under the wings of the Shechinah.

---

Translation: The Soncino Talmud

This source can be found online at www.sefaria.org and https://halakhah.com.

# Appendix C

## Fable of the Goat

### S.Y. Agnon

The tale is told of an old man who groaned
from his heart. The doctors were sent for, and they
advised him to drink goat's milk. He went out and
bought a she-goat and brought her into his home.
Not many days passed before the goat disappeared.
They went out to search for her but did not find
her. She was not in the yard and not in the garden,
not on the roof of the house of study and not by
the spring, not in the hills and not in the fields. She
tarried several days and then returned by herself;
and when she returned, her udder was full of a
great deal of milk, the taste of which was as the
taste of Eden. Not just once, but many times she
disappeared from the house. They would go out
in search of her and would not find her until she
returned by herself with her udder full of milk that
was sweeter than honey and whose taste was the
taste of Eden.

One time the old man said to his son, "My son,
I desire to know where she goes and whence she
brings this milk which is sweet to my palate and a
balm to all my bones."

His son said to him, "Father, I have a plan."

He said to him, "What is it?"

The son got up and brought a length of cord. He tied it to the goat's tail.

His father said to him, "What are you doing, my son?"

He said to him, "I am tying a cord to the goat's tail, so that when I feel a pull on it I will know that she has decided to leave, and I can catch the end of the cord and follow her on her way." The old man nodded his head and said to him, "My son, if your heart is wise, my heart too will rejoice."

The youth tied the cord to the goat's tail and minded it carefully. When the goat set off, he held the cord in his hand and did not let it slacken until the goat was well on her way and he was following her. He was dragged along behind her until he came to a cave. The goat went into the cave, and the youth followed her, holding the cord. They walked thus for an hour or two, or maybe even a day or two. The goat wagged her tail and bleated, and the cave came to an end.

When they emerged from the cave, the youth saw lofty mountains, and hills full of the choicest fruit, and a fountain of living waters that flowed down from the mountains; and the wind wafted all manner of perfumes. The goat climbed up a tree by clutching at the ribbed leaves. Carob fruits full of honey dropped from the tree, and she ate of the carobs and drank of the garden's fountain.

The youth stood and called to the wayfarers: "I adjure you, good people, tell me where I am, and what is the name of this place?"

They answered him, "You are in the Land of Israel, and you are close by Safed."

The youth lifted up his eyes to the heavens and said, "Blessed be the Omnipresent, blessed be He who has brought me to the Land of Israel." He kissed the soil and sat down under the tree.

He said, "Until the day breathe and the shadows flee away, I shall sit on the hill under this tree. Then I shall go home and bring my father and mother to the Land of Israel." As he was sitting thus and feasting his eyes on the holiness of the Land of Israel, he heard a voice proclaiming: "Come, let us go out to greet the Sabbath Queen."

And he saw men like angels, wrapped in white shawls, with boughs of myrtle in their hands, and all the houses were lit with a great many candles. He perceived that the eve of Sabbath would arrive with the darkening, and that he would not be able to return.

He uprooted a reed and dipped it in gallnuts, from which the ink for the writing of the Torah scrolls is made. He took a piece of paper and wrote a letter to his father: "From the ends of the earth I lift up my voice in song to tell you that I have come in peace to the Land of Israel. Here I sit, close by Safed, the holy city, and I imbibe its sanctity. Do not inquire how I arrived here but hold on to this cord which is tied to the goat's tail and follow the footsteps of the goat; then your journey will be secure, and you will enter the Land of Israel."

The youth rolled up the note and placed it in the goat's ear. He said to himself: When she arrives at Father's house, Father will pat her on the head, and she will flick her ears. The note will fall out, Father will pick it up and read what is written on it. Then he will take up the cord and follow the goat to the Land of Israel.

The goat returned to the old man, but she did not flick her ears, and the note did not fall. When the old man saw that the goat had returned without his son, he clapped his hands to his head and began to cry and weep and wail, "My son, my son, where are you? My son, would that I might die in your stead, my son, my son."

So he went, weeping and mourning over his son, for he said, "An evil beast has devoured him, my son is assuredly rent in pieces!"

And he refused to be comforted, saying, "I will go down to my grave in mourning for my son."

And whenever he saw the goat, he would say, "Woe to the father who banished his son, and woe to her who drove him from the world!"

The old man's mind would not be at peace until he sent for the butcher to slaughter the goat. The butcher came and slaughtered the goat. As they were skinning her, the note fell out of her ear. The old man picked up the note and said, "My son's handwriting!"

When he had read all that his son had written, he clapped his hands to his head and cried, "*Vay! Vay!* Woe to the man who robs himself of his own good fortune, and woe to the man who requites good with evil!"

He mourned over the goat many days and

refused to be comforted, saying, "Woe to me, for I could have gone up to the Land of Israel in one bound, and now I must suffer out my days in this exile!"

Since that time the mouth of the cave has been hidden from the eye, and there is no longer a short way. And that youth, if he has not died, shall bear fruit in his old age, full of sap and richness, calm and peaceful in the Land of the Living.

*– Translated by Barney Rubin*

# From Foe to Friend

## *S.Y. Agnon*

Before Talpiot was built the King of the
Winds used to rule over the entire region; and all
his ministers and servants, mighty and stubborn
winds, dwelled there with him and blew over
mountain and valley, hill and ravine, doing
whatever their hearts desired, as if the land had
been given to them alone.

I went out there once and saw how lovely the
place was – the air crisp, the sky pure blue, the
land so open and free – and I strolled around a bit.
A wind accosted me. "What are you doing here?"
he said to me. "I'm taking a walk," I said. "Ah, so
you're taking a walk?" he said. He clapped me on
the head and sent my hat flying. I bent down to
pick it up. He rumpled my coat, turned it upside
down over my head, and made a fool of me. I
pulled my coat back off my head. He came at me
again, knocked me to the ground and roared with
wild laughter. I got to my feet and stood straight.
He bumped up against me and shouted: "On your
way! On your way!"

I saw I couldn't contend with one mightier
than myself, and I went on my way.

I returned to the city and went inside my
house. I became restless and went out. Whether
I intended it or not, my feet carried me back to
Talpiot. I remembered all that the wind had done
to me. I took some canvas and pegs and pitched a

tent for myself – a refuge from wind and storm.

One night I stayed there. The light suddenly went out. I left the tent to see who had put my light out. I found the wind standing outside. "What do you want?" I asked him. He boxed my ears and slapped my mouth. I went back into my tent. He pulled up my tent pegs and split my rope, turned my tent over and ripped my canvas to shreds. He turned upon me as well and almost knocked me over.

I saw I couldn't possibly match his strength. I picked up my feet and went back to the city. I went back to the city and remained within its walls. I became restless and yearned for some place with fresh, pleasant air. Since there is no air anywhere in the entire land like the air of Talpiot, I went to Talpiot. And so that the wind wouldn't abuse me, I took some boards with me and made myself a hut. I thought I had found myself a resting place, but the wind thought otherwise. A day hardly passed before he started thumping on my roof and shaking the walls. One night he carried off the whole hut.

The wind carried off my hut and left me without any shelter. I picked myself up and went back to the city.

What happened to me once and then a second time happened to me a third time. I returned to the city and I had no peace. How my heart drew me to that very spot from which I had been driven out!

I said to my heart: "Don't you see that is impossible for us to return to a place from which we have been chased away? And what is impossible is impossible." But my heart thought differently. If I said a thousand times, *Impossible!* my heart replied a thousand and one times, *It is possible!*

I took wood and stones and built myself a house.

I won't praise my house, for it was small; but I am not ashamed of it, even though there are bigger and better houses. My house was small, but there was room enough in my house for a man like me who doesn't desire grandeur.

The wind saw that I had built myself a house. He came and asked me:

"What is this?"

"This is a house," I said to him.

He laughed and said: "I'll be damned if I ever saw anything as funny as this thing you call a house!"

I too laughed and said: "What you have never seen before, you see before you now."

He laughed and said: "What is it, this house?"

I laughed and said: "A house is... a house!"

He laughed and said to me: "I'll go and inspect it."

He stretched out his hand and inspected the door. The door broke and fell. He stretched out his hand and inspected the windows. The windows broke and fell. Finally he rose and went to the roof. Up he went and down came the roof. The wind laughed at me and said:

"Where is this house you built?"

I too asked where my house was. But I didn't laugh.

At first when the wind drove me away I used to return to the city. Finally things happened that prevented me from returning to the city. Like a homeless animal, I did not know where to go. To return to the city was impossible because of what had happened there; to return to Talpiot was impossible because of the wind who drove me out. I had made myself a tent and a hut but they hadn't lasted. I had built myself a little house, but that hadn't stood up to the wind either. But then, maybe it hadn't withstood the wind because it was so small and frail; perhaps if it had been big and strong it would have stood. I took strong timber and sturdy beams, large blocks of stone, plaster and cement, and I hired good workers and watched over their work day and night. This time I was wise enough to sink the foundations very deep. The house was built and it stood firm and upright on its own ground. When the house was finished the wind came and thumped on the shutters.

"Who is rapping on my window?" I asked.

He laughed playfully and said: "A neighbor."

"What does one neighbor want of another on a night of storm and tempest like this?" I asked him.

He laughed and said: "He has come to wish his neighbor well in his new house."

"Is it usual for a neighbor to come through the window like a thief?" I said to him.

He came around and knocked on the door.

"Who is rapping on my door?" I said to him.

"It is I, your neighbor," said the wind.

"You are my neighbor – please come in," I said.

"But the door is locked," he said to me.

"Well, if the door is locked, it must be because I locked it," I said to him.

"Open up!" the wind answered.

"I'm sensitive to the cold, wait till the sun comes up and I will let you in," I said.

When the sun rose I went out to let him in but I couldn't find him. I stood in front of my house and saw that the land was desolate all around: not a tree, not a green leaf anywhere; only dust and stones. "I'll plant a garden here," I said to myself.

I took a spade and started digging. When the soil was ready I brought some saplings. The rains came and watered the saplings; the dews came, and the saplings sprouted; the sun nourished them, and they blossomed. Not many days passed before the saplings that I had planted became trees with many branches.

I made myself a bench and sat in the shade of the trees.

One night the wind returned and started knocking the trees about. What did the trees do? They struck back at him. The wind rose again and shook the trees. Once more the trees struck in return. The wind lost his breath. He turned and went away.

From that time on the wind has been quite humble and meek, and when he comes he behaves like a gentleman. And since he minds his manners with me, I too mind my manners with him. When he comes I go out to meet him and ask him to sit with me on the garden bench beneath the trees. And he comes and sits by my side. And when he comes he brings with him a pleasant scent from the mountains and valleys, and he fans the air gently around me. Since he behaves like a complete penitent, I never remind him of his former wicked ways.

And when he leaves me and goes on his way I invite him to come again, as one should with a good neighbor. And we really are the best of neighbors, and I am very fond of him. And he may even be fond of me.

– *Translated by Joel Blocker*

# Acknowledgements

*Avraham Infeld*

During the last few years, I have been honored four times with the receipt of either a prize or an honorary doctorate from an academic institution. On each of those occasions, I felt very awkward being the only one among all those honored who had written neither a book nor a check. Well, I have now tried to write a book; I still can't afford to write a sizeable check. I am, however, a very, very wealthy person, not in any particular currency but in family, friends, colleagues, and fellow travelers with whom I have lived and still live. I owe them immense gratitude.

First, to my wife, Ellen. Probably the most un-American American I have ever met: quiet, introverted, honest, and always there for me and our children. She has served me as an anchor, keeping me grounded while allowing me neither enough rope to hang myself nor too little to restrain my constantly demanding curiosity. I could have achieved nothing without the knowledge that behind me there was a home and family that she ensured were always well taken care of. I doubt there is anyone to whom I owe more gratitude.

I have one sibling – my sister, Tamara – eight years older than me but, without a doubt, the closest friend anyone could wish for. She is very different from me. We are like two separate branches of the same tree with common roots. She was born four years before the Holocaust, and I was born four years before the creation of the State of Israel. Her first years of awareness were of a saddened and troubled Jewish People. My first years of awareness were rooted in the joy of the creation of Israel. I have always counted on her counsel and hope to do so for many years to come.

To my children, Aylon, Avital, Ami, and Anat, thank you for inspiring me each day by living lives of commitment to the past, understanding of the present, and hope for the future. I have no doubt that you, my grandchildren, and the generations to follow will ensure the continued significant renaissance of the Jewish People.

Boy, did I know how to choose parents! So much love, so much concern, so many lessons, and so much support. No child has ever made a better choice of parents and they were so central to my life and play an important role in the book itself.

While I mention very few colleagues in the book, I have been blessed to work with educators and educational administrators of the highest caliber and from all walks of Jewish life. If I mention any, I know I will miss out others who should have been mentioned. You all know who you are. Whether we worked together at Ulpan Akiva, the Jewish Agency, Melitz, Taglit Birthright Israel, Hillel, the Chais Foundation, or Reut, I would not be me were it not for what I learned from all of you.

I do, however, want to mention one colleague and that is Clare Goldwater, who wrote this book with me. She has been an avid listener, an acute interrogator, and an artful articulator, and people tell me that she has captured my voice perfectly. Her commitment to getting this book published has been unbelievable.

Ami Infeld, despite being my son, is now the CEO of Melitz, an organization that has committed itself to bringing this book to fruition. It was Melitz that inspired so many friends and philanthropists to enable this publication. To my very dear friends Sandy Baklor, Arlene Kaufman, and Julie Wise Oreck, who led the campaign, I tip my hat. And to all those that I haven't mentioned, you know who you are, I know who you are, and you forever have a place in my heart. Many thanks to all.

Jerusalem, October 2017

# Acknowledgements

*Clare Goldwater*

Little did I know when I began my professional journey in Jewish education that I would somehow be accompanied by Avraham Infeld through all the years and in many different ways. From my first interactions as a participant in Melitz programs, as an educator working for the organization, and as a Board member, I was enormously influenced by his contribution to experiential Jewish education. Later, after he recruited me to work for him at Hillel in Washington DC, I really got to know him and appreciate his leadership and generosity of spirit. And then, when I returned to Israel, I was lucky enough to find myself working with him on an article, which later turned into this book.

The idea of writing a book seemed rather mysterious and risky at first. Neither of us was sure how it was going to look, or exactly how it would turn out. But we started talking – or rather, he started talking and I listened and asked questions. There followed two years of (almost) weekly meetings. We started with the most familiar and well-known stories and ideas and kept digging deeper into new territory, capturing ideas that weren't always fully-formed or were less familiar even to those who know Avraham well.

For me this process has been nothing but a privilege. I don't have the words to express how grateful I am to have been able to sit in Avraham's study and encourage him to tell stories, to think, and to turn the long years of his career into lessons for the rest of us. He has made me laugh and cry, we have argued and debated, and he has shared his ideas generously with me.

Avraham, you write about the many wonderful people who were your teachers and mentors. If and when I ever come to write a book about my ideas, you will surely be there as one of my most important teachers. I am so grateful. Thank you for letting me be there to listen and learn from you. I hope I have done justice to your ideas.

I also want to thank my family for enabling me to be where I am today. To my parents, who instilled in me a deep sense of belonging and commitment to the Jewish People, and are still rather bemused that it all turned out this way. To Jeremy, for being my partner, my support, my friend, and for listening, reading, provoking and always inspiring me to be the best I can be. And to Elisheva, for whose future all our efforts are made.

Jerusalem, October 2017

# Acknowledgements

*Ami Infeld, CEO Melitz*

In the early 1970s, young people all over the world were questioning heretofore-unchallenged assumptions. In the context of those times, a group of Israeli high school students who were about to be drafted for their compulsory army service wrote a letter to then Prime Minister Golda Meir, asking why they were putting their lives on the line for the State of Israel. Prime Minister Meir, shocked by their lack of knowledge about the Jewish historical connections to the people and land of Israel, approached Jewish educational leaders for solutions. It is against this backdrop that Melitz was created.

Thanks to the efforts of its talented staff, under Avraham Infeld's leadership, Melitz grew to be in the forefront of the development of educational tools and opportunities for Jews of all ages, producing unique and diverse programs and training, promoting a Jewish and democratic vision of Israel with strong connections to Jewish world-wide.

It is only natural therefore that Melitz assume the responsibility of publishing this book which reflects so much of Melitz's educational doctrine.

I would like to thank everyone who worked towards the success of this project. Firstly, Clare Goldwater, who over a two-year period devoted unbelievable efforts to capturing both Avraham's ideas and his voice; Nikki Littman, our editor, who managed to both edit and leave Avraham's "voice" present in the text; Jen Klor for her unique and wonderful design; the Melitz board and staff, all the consultants and in particular the friends who read versions of the manuscript and generously shared their feedback; Esther Abramowitz, Jonny Ariel, Shoshana Boyd Gelfand, Scott Copeland, Elan Ezrachi, Gidi Grinstein, Yonatan Mirvis and Gidi Shimoni.

Please share your feedback about the book and connect to the educational initiatives that are related to it. Connect with us at www.melitz.org.

# Special Thanks from Melitz

A special thanks to the funders, under the leadership of Sandy Baklor, Arlene Kaufman and Julie Wise Oreck, who helped bring this project to fruition. By your designated gift to the publication of the book, its Hebrew translation and the "5 Legged Table" curriculum that will follow, you ensured that Avraham Infeld's teachings will reach as wide an audience as possible.

# In Particular, Our Thanks To:

Laurie Blitzer

Bonnie and David Brand, Virginia Beach, VA

Andrea and Charles Bronfman Philanthropies

Diane and Kenneth Feinberg

Beth Kaplan and Bruce Sholk

Keith Krivitzky

Stuart Kurlander

Laura and Gary Lauder

Mark Levy

Suzy and David Liebman

Brian Lurie

Kathy Manning and Randall Kaplan

Joseph Meyerhoff Fund, Inc

Pearlstone Family Fund (Jewish Community Federation
of Baltimore)

Ben and Esther Rosenblum Foundation

Susan & Alan Rothenberg

Charles & Lynn Schusterman Family Foundation

Jodi J. Schwartz

Cindy and David Shapira

Jane and Larry Sherman

Carole A. Solomon Fund

Jane and Mark Wilf

Carol B. Wise

Diane Wohl

The Endowment Fund of the Jewish Federation of Cleveland

Photo: Max Orenstein

Based in Jerusalem, but a tireless traveler to all parts of the globe, Avraham Infeld has dedicated his long and distinguished career to helping Jews find meaning and joy in their Jewish identities.

Born in South Africa and raised in a strongly Zionist family, Avraham made *aliyah* to Israel and studied Jewish History and Bible at the Hebrew University, and Law at Tel Aviv University. Embarking thereafter on what would become a career in Jewish education, Avraham served among other roles in the following leadership positions:

- Program Director at Ulpan Akiva
- First Community Shaliach in the US, serving Baltimore and Washington
- Founder and President of Melitz Centers of Jewish Zionist Education
- Director of Shalom Hartman Institute
- Director of the Jewish Agency for Israel's Youth Department for English-Speaking Europe
- Director of Planning Process of Taglit Birthright Israel
- International President and CEO of Hillel: The Foundation for Jewish Campus Life
- President of the Chais Family Foundation
- Mentor to the Reut Institute for Tikkun Olam and Jewish Peoplehood

In recognition of his contributions to Jewish education, Avraham is the recipient of the Hebrew University's prestigious Samuel Rothberg Prize for Jewish Education, Hillel's Renaissance Award, and honorary doctorates from Muhlenberg College and Hebrew Union College – Jewish Institute of Religion.

**Clare Goldwater** is an educational consultant and leadership coach who works with organizations and professionals to expand their potential.

Born in the UK, she was inspired to contribute to the Jewish world by her experiences with Jewish student activism. She made *aliyah* and been working in Jewish education ever since, as a tour guide, educator, coach and consultant.

Upon graduating from the Jerusalem Fellows program at the Mandel Leadership Institute Avraham Infeld recruited Clare to Hillel in Washington DC, where she became the Vice President for Jewish Experience responsible for developing educational strategy and creating systems and programs to bring meaningful Jewish experiences to students across North America.

Clare has a B.A. from Oxford University, an M.A. in Education from the Hebrew University and is a graduate of the Leadership Coaching Program at Georgetown University. She has served on the boards of Melitz, Hazon, Ayeka and was a co-founder of the Sela Public Charter School in Washington, DC.

For the past decade she has worked with a portfolio of organizations and professionals in Israel, Europe and North America. She lives in Jerusalem with her family.

CPSIA information can be obtained
at www.ICGtesting.com
Printed in the USA
FFOW04n1511010318
45373940-46050FF